ACTS 29ERS INTERNATIONAL:
&
'POINT 2 POINT WITH JESUS:'
MINISTRIES

"FULFILLING YOUR POTENTIAL IN CHRIST:"

BARRIE J. ROWLAND-HORNBLOW:
PASTOR ('RE-TYRED')

"A CALEB PUBLICATION"

FOREWORD TO THIS BOOK:

The reader will only get out of this book, 'Fulfilling Your Potential in Christ' the truths of His Word, To the extent of your openness To receive from God and then to continue 'Walking in the Light of God's Word' Psalm 119:105;

This book 'Fulfilling Your Potential in Christ.' is the culminations of 'House group commentary on the original manuscript, based on Psalm 119v105; and is designed for House meetings where there are new or recently converted attendees present and for private study.

As it has with me personally, I believe that it is also good for all Christians to refresh themselves in the fundamental of our Faith.

- Indicates Quotable quotes which have blessed me during the past 50 years of Ministry.

Scripture is from the New Living Translation (NLT.) unless otherwise noted.

Copyright @ 2025 by Barrie J. Rowland-Hornblow

All rights reserved. No part of this book may be reproduced in any manner whatsoever without the express permission of the publisher except in the case of brief quotations for a book review or other scholarly journal.

ISBN: 978-0-6459827-4-9

CONTENTS:

Chapter	Page
Salvation Eternal Life Experience	4
Authority of God's Word	13
Water Baptism	21
Enabling of the Holy Spirit	29
Introduction to the Spiritual Gifts	42
The Nine Gifts Explained	53
Established in the Church	66
A Greater Gift	77
Dynamics of the Vocal Gifts	89
Tithing and Offerings	100

Chapter One:
'SALVATION, AN 'ETERNAL LIFE' EXPERIENCE.'

John 3:16; K.J.V. *'For God so loved the world that he gave his only begotten son, that whosoever believes on him should not perish but have everlasting life.'*

*THE FOUNDATION OF GOD'S LOVE IS CLEARLY SEEN IN ALL OF HIS CREATION.

When we love someone, it can always be measured by the degree of sacrifice or cost we are willing to place upon ourselves, without conditions. This truly is an unconditional love, Selfless, and without strings.

A lesson I learnt as a child, but I only understood when the ramifications of the price became so high, it forced me to become accountable for my actions, was that:

*'FOR EVERY CAUSE, THERE IS AN EFFECT.'

Sin is the cause of our separation from God, and the consequential effect is always death. This is an irreversible law in all things.

We do well to remember that sin – that is – a broken relationship with God, has always led to guilt and to condemnation, resulting conclusively in death. God has given us a way, by and through which we can renew our fellowship – that means relationship – with Him.

Genesis tells us that God made man in His own image, pure and without fault. Therefore, God has given us a way in which the price has been paid, in full, for our redemption.

He gave us the only way, and that is through our believing in Jesus Christ, who is after all, 'the Son of the Living God.'

John 1:12; *'But to as many as did receive Him, to those who put their trust in His person and power, He gave the right (power) to become children of God. Not because of bloodline, physical impulse, or human intention but because of God.'* complete Jewish Bible. Author: David H. Stern.

When we receive Christ as our personal saviour, we automatically receive in ourselves, His Spirit. We are born again as of that moment in time. We also received within us, His power.

Power is translated in two distinct ways in the Greek.

The first way is as above with the Greek word *Exousia*, which translates to, executive or authority.

And the second is Dunamis which has the meaning of Dynamic or Ability. Thus, we have a being: Exousia and a doing: Dunamis.

Acts 1:8; KJV. *'But you shall receive power, after that the Holy Ghost is come upon you: and you shall be witnesses unto me both in Jerusalem, and in all Judaea, and in Samaria, and unto the uttermost part of the earth.'*

- *'JOHN 1:12; IS THE POWER TO BE: EXOUSIA. ACTS 1:8; IS THE POWER TO DO: DUNAMIS.'*

This authority or power entitles us to call ourselves and live as sons of the King with total assurance that we are acting according to our inheritance. We in effect become the King's Kids.

The authority and power are in His name and is given to us through our believing and receiving of Jesus as our personal saviour. There is no other way.

When we look for easier ways of doing things, we often discover that the easy, comfortable ways, do not always produce the positive outcome which we desire.

Until it becomes very clear to us that we need to change our ways, we can feel sorry for ourselves – The Blame Game Mentality – or we can determine to change our behaviour. The choice is always up to us.

There is an old saying which I heard many years ago. It sounds corny but it contains a hard truth.

* *'THERE ARE NO FREE LUNCHES.'*

Surely if God could have found another way to redeem us from our sin, He would have found it. The price to be paid was the highest of all because the sins of the world, that is yours and mine, as well as all that has gone before, and that which is yet to come, had an eternal price tag, and God knew that, and bought us with the greatest gift of all – His Son.

Jesus is the eternal sacrifice, paid out in full, so that we may receive eternal life, in Him. This new position of authority is not, gradual, it is a now time situational, 'as we believe so we receive.'

In the Scripture John 1:12; mentioned above, we have the word *'become'* which means 'to express an immediate change.'

- *'OFF WITH THE OLD LIFE*
- *ON WITH THE NEW LIFE.'*

The following passage is the first passage I learnt in the first week of my Christian life.

Therefore, what I received then, I have pleasure sharing with you now, some 51 years later. I can, truthfully say, that the truths in this passage have given me the confidence to walk continually In Him.

John 3:1-21; NLT. *'There was a man named Nicodemus, a Jewish religious leader who was a Pharisee. After dark one evening, he came to speak with Jesus.*

'Rabbi' he said, 'We all know that God has sent you to teach us. Your miraculous signs are evidence that God is with you.'

Jesus replied, 'I tell you the truth, unless you are born again, you cannot see the Kingdom of God.'

'What do you mean?' exclaimed Nicodemus. 'How can an old man go back into his mother's womb and be born again?'

Jesus replied, 'I assure you; no one can enter the Kingdom of God without being born of water and the Spirit. Humans can reproduce only human life, but the Holy Spirit gives birth to spiritual life. So do not be surprised when I say, 'You must be born again.

The wind blows wherever it wants. Just as you can hear the wind but cannot tell where it comes from or where it is going, so you cannot explain how people are born of the Spirit.'

'How are these things possible?' Nicodemus asked.

7

Jesus replied, 'You are a respected Jewish teacher, and yet you do not understand these things? I assure you; we tell you what we know and have seen, and yet you will not believe our testimony. But if you do not believe me when I tell you about earthly things, how can you possibly believe if I tell you about heavenly things?

No one has ever gone to heaven and returned. But the Son of Man has come down from heaven. And as Moses lifted the bronze snake on a pole in the wilderness, so the Son of Man must be lifted so that everyone who believes in him will have eternal life.

For this is how God loved the world: He gave his one and only Son, so that everyone who believes in him will not perish but have eternal life. God sent his Son into the world not to judge the world, but to save the world through him. There is no judgement against anyone who believes in him.

But anyone who does not believe in him has already been judged for not believing in God's one and only Son. And the judgement is based on this fact:

God's light came into the world, but people loved the darkness more than the light, for their actions were evil. All who do evil hate the light and refuse to go near it for fear their sins will be exposed. But those who do what is right come to the light so others can see that they are doing what God wants.'

There is only one way to see and understand the things of God, and that is to see through the Spirit of God, which comes when we accept and thereby receive his Son and become 'born again.'

There is only one way to gain for our self, the goal of Eternal Life, and that is by doing it God's way rather than the futile efforts of the ways of man.

Along time ago – those were the days in the beginning of my Christian Walk – I wrote a note to myself, believing that God was speaking to me, and that if I wrote it down in my bible, I would never forget it.

'RELIGIOSITY AND CHURCHIANITY, ARE MANKIND'S' WAYS TO FIND THEIR GOD. CHRISTIANITY, IS GOD'S WAY FOR HIS PEOPLE TO FIND AND RESTORE RELATIONSHIP WITH HIM.'

This notation has given me an ongoing principal by which I can honestly encourage you to have in your procession a Bible that is good enough to write in when God speaks to you.

IF WE ARE ONLY BORN ONCE; Natural birth from our mother's womb, protected in a water sack, THEN WE WILL DIE TWICE; physically and at judgement.

IF WE ARE BORN TWICE; from our mother's womb, and our New Creation experience – of water and the spirit, respectively. THEN WE SHALL ONLY DIE ONCE. naturally.

    1. Those who receive Christ, do not hope, they know that they have eternal life.

    2. Eternal life is not something after our body is dead and buried.

It is however, what the believer has in the now time life, that – he or she – lives in Jesus. In effect Eternal life begins in the now time of our true conversion to Christ, and our consequential relationship with God is restored.

This is because God has a NOW TIME CLOCK and from the moment of your conversion you have IN HIM HIS FOREVER NOW TIME forever.

This means that we continue in 'Eternity' from that time on – both in the here and now of Kingdom living – and is therefore living in that Eternity by faith in Jesus and continually into the life beyond.

    3. When we receive Christ as our personal Saviour, we do not become a religious person, but we do become a child of the Living God and therefore an inheritor of the kingdom.

    4. We become a child of the Living God, not because of our efforts, but by the Grace of God who gave up His Son to die on the cross for our sins.

It is His sacrifice that enables us to claim the inheritance and the assurance we receive, currently, because He has already paid the ultimate price on our behalf.

I share with you a story that was told to me early in my Christian Walk and is now a constant reminder to me of this Truth.

A criminal – that is me or you – are found guilty of the crime committed and is imprisoned for as long as the penalty price, let us say in today's terms, One Trillion Dollars, remains unpaid.

The prisoner knows, because he knows, because he knows, that there is no way he can pay that price, therefore he accepts the reality of a lifelong sentence without remission, and without any sort of parole. He expects therefore to remain in that incarcerated state for ever.

Then a stranger appeals to the court and pays the total cost – the bible calls it the redemption price – and the jailer comes to turn the key and opens the prison gate releasing – me or you – from the prison.

Now let us consider that the prisoner did not believe in miracles and refused to walk out of his prison cell. He would be thinking all kinds of strange things, such as a conspiracy, a trap, and the like, so to speak. He just could not believe that someone, who was a total stranger to him, would do such a thing.

Nevertheless, the penalty price has been paid in full, the prison door has been unlocked and you and I are free to walk out of that prison, a brand-new person – A New Creation.

Corinthians 5:17-19; KJV. *'Therefore, if any man be in Christ, he is a new creature: old things are passed away; behold, all things are become new.*

And all things are of God, who has reconciled us to himself by Jesus Christ, and has given to us the ministry of reconciliation;

To wit, that God was in Christ, reconciling the world unto himself, not imputing their trespasses unto them; and hath committed unto us the word of reconciliation.'

5. We believe that we are a child of God and have eternal life, not because of our feeling state, nor indeed because our pastor told us so. But we believe that we are born again because the Bible, God's word, states it as a fact.

"GOD SAID IT, I BELIEVE IT, THAT SETTLES IT WITH ME."

Chapter Two:
"THE AUTHORITY OF GOD'S WORD – THE BIBLE."

2 Timothy 3:14-17; NLT. *'But you must remain faithful to the things you have been taught. You know they are true, for you know you can trust those who taught you.*

You have been taught the holy Scriptures from childhood, and they have given you the wisdom to receive the salvation that comes by trusting in Christ Jesus.

All Scripture is inspired by God and is useful to teach us what is true and to make us realise what is wrong in our lives. It corrects us when we are wrong and teaches us to do what is right. God uses it to prepare and equip his people to do every good work.'

It is important that we see the Bible as, the 'Word of God.'

It is also important that we see its truth, not only in what it contains, but also in and by the very nature of the Author Himself. This verse tells us the function of the Bible and divides it into four areas of daily living.

1. DOCTRINE: This means teaching.
2. REPROOF: This means to convict and is a measure by which testing occurs.
3. CORRECTION: Always used by God so that we may improve both our life and character.
4. INSTRUCTION IN RIGHTEOUSNESS: By which we can, after seeing the error of our ways walk along a new path with God, as was His original purpose of our creation.

The word righteous means simply to walk in good and favourable standing with both God and our fellow man. We do this when we follow in the ways and instructions of the Lord. These instructions are given to us in God inspired writings which we call the Bible. This does not exclude human involvement, because in the very beginning God 'created man in his own image' that he might have such involvement and intimacy one with another.

The reality of verses 16 and 17 is very clear. He has given us the tools and we need to learn how to use them. Because verse 16 has given to us the function of God's Word, then verse 17 clearly lays out the purposes of God's word.

It is God's desire and design that we should live in perfect harmony with Him.

Not only does He state the goal, He, equips us for the journey, so to speak. What a caring and wonderful God we serve, as we learn to 'Fulfilling Your Potential in Christ '

So then, 2Timothy 3:16 & 17 are the two verses which become the foundation from which we will be able to discern God's will for our individual lives, thus allowing His living word to work in and through us.

The following Scripture reveals the central theme of a Christian – follower of Jesus – life.

I know this because I can testify that this passage has been the parameter within which I have been transformed from my B.C. (before Christ) to my present AD. (in Christ), life.

Proverbs 4:20-27; NLT. *'My child, pay attention to what I say. Listen carefully to my words. Do not lose sight of them. Let them penetrate deep into your heart, for they bring life to those who find them, and healing to their whole body. Guard your heart above all else, for it determines the course of your life.*

Avoid all perverse talk; stay away from corrupt speech. Look straight ahead and fix your eyes on what lies before you. Mark out a straight path for your feet; stay on the safe path. Do not get side-tracked; keep your feet from following evil.'

If we were to catalogue the above passage of Scripture, it would look like this:

Pay attention –
    Carefully consider –
        Hold fast –
            Absorb deep –
                Determine to follow–
Health to your whole being –
    Activate protective strategy –
        avoid negativity –
            determine your course,
                Above all things do not get side-tracked FROM YOUR GOAL.

God set man apart from the rest of his Creation. This is the spiritual aspect of man which allows him the right to have fellowship and communion with his creator.

Genesis 1:26a; KJV. *'God said, "Let Us make man in Our Own image, after Our Own likeness.'*

This then, is the perfect creation and the perfect will He has for us, righteousness personified.

Genesis 1:28a; KJV. *'And God blessed them, and God said to them, be fruitful, multiply and replenish and subdue the earth and all that is contained therein.'*

A: God's will for us, is that we should be fully equipped to do the work of the ministry.

B: If we truly intend and desire to follow Christ Jesus as Lord and Saviour, then these two verses will become a platform from which such desires and aspirations will flow.

* *'FROM GLORY TO GLORY, HE IS CHANGING ME.'*

Joshua 1:8-9; KJV. *'This book of the law shall not depart out of your mouth, but you shall meditate therein both day and night, that you may observe to do all that it contains.*

For then you shall make your way prosperous and then you shall have good success. Have I not commanded you, be strong and of good courage; be not afraid, nor be dismayed; for the Lord your God is with you wherever you may go.'

C: God's Word is full of promises; He alone is bound to make good. However, we have a significant part to play in the order of things. We must follow the rules and guidelines which He has laid down for us.

D: We must meditate – that is to read, digest and dwell on what the Bible states – because only in God's word lies all our answers for the daily situations common to all. It is in this, the word of God, that we find the solutions to the personal problems we face in this materialistic world.

E: Because our answers are contained in God's Word then it is logical that we learn to use it, the Word of God, for our own benefit and to God's glory.

F: Using the word of God is the only method by which we, as God's children, and therefore inheritors of the kingdom, can take hold of the 'promised land.'

*'SALVATION IS THE GATEWAY, THE WORD IS OUR WEAPON, THE WORLD IS OUR DOMINION, WHEN WE CLAIM JESUS AS OUR LORD.'

*Psalm 119:105; KJV *'Your word, Lord, is a lamp to my feet and a light to my pathway.'*

The Word of God not only shows us where we are by the immediacy of the lamp, but also guides our directions by the beam of the light. My foundational teacher was the late, Pastor Lyle Potts of the New Life Centre Fellowship in Moe Victoria, and he taught me that God's Word was a personal letter to me. Therefore, God speaks to me in my language, so to speak, and thus the following is my understanding of this verse.

Psalm 119: 105; BJR-H. *'Lord, your word is a lamp to my feet so that I may see where I am, and firmness for my feet – the security, the rock, upon which I am assured and given confidence.*

And your word is also the light to show me the path upon which you would have me walk.

Therefore, giving me the confidence that my future pathway is under your guidance, which is found in the Scriptures – your word to me – set before me.'

The real need in the life of a Christian is the security of the Word of God that will enable us to have confidence when we are called into service.

We can always have confidence to exercise our faith when we are guided by the eternal and absolute light of the gospel, which can only be found, in Him.

John 6:63; KJV. *'It is the spirit that makes alive, the flesh profits nothing. The words that I speak to you, they are spirit, and they are life.'*

The Word of God dwells in the heart of man, in the spirit. The mind of man will never live profitably in the things of God unless, or until it is, 'renewed from the spirit.'

The Bible is the Word of the Living God and therefore needs to be lived in to be effective.

Romans 12:2; KJV. *'And be not conformed to this world, but be transformed by the renewing of your mind, that you may prove what is that good, and acceptable, and perfect will, of God.'*

God has in His wisdom allowed us to choose, allowed us to make decisions about what we do both in and with our personal lives.

If we chose to be controlled by this world and its ways then that is our choice, and we must accept the consequences of such decisions. Every cause has an effect, but God has given us a new and better way to live. He gave us His Son Jesus to show us the Way and the Truth and the Life. Through Him all things are possible.

We still make the decisions about what we do and where we go, but we chose to follow the Directions which God has laid out before us in His Word, the Bible. This is in reality:

> *'THE LIGHT FOR THE WORLD.
> IS THE LIGHTHOUSE OF SALVATION.'*

The Light, which is ever constant, and which shines before us, so that in absolute confidence we can clearly see the pathway and enjoy a life of success and enjoyment.

> *'I MUST SEEK THE LORD OF THE WORD,
> BEFORE THE WORD OF THE LORD
> CAN EFFECT
> A CHANGE, IN ME.'*

So far you, the reader, will have read of two very important lessons concerning the Christian beliefs. The way is now open for you – if you have not already done so – to receive the Lord Jesus as your personal Saviour.

If you have already done so then you should be encouraged to walk as a Christian ought, upright and confident, in victory and in that righteousness which comes from your relationship with God and those around you.

For those of you who have not yet accepted Jesus as your personal Saviour and declared Him to be the Lord of your life, the invitation is now given to pray with me as you read the following prayer.

"DEAR LORD JESUS, I INVITED YOU TO ENTER INTO MY LIFE AND SHINE YOUR LIGHT EVER BEFORE ME. I ASK YOU TO FORGIVE ME FOR THE WRONGS I HAVE DONE, THE SINS WHICH I HAVE COMMITTED AND WASH ME AFRESH, WITH THE WORD OF LIFE.

AS I PRAY TO YOU THIS DAY,
I ASK THAT YOU BE MY CONSTANT COMPANION, FRIEND, COUNSELLOR, AND GUIDE,
FOR THE REST OF MY LIFE.

I MAKE THIS COMMITMENT TO YOU BECAUSE OF THE REALISATION THAT THE STEP OF FAITH IS MINE TO DO, AND THE AUTHORITY OF THE WORD IS YOURS TO GIVE.

THANK YOU, JESUS, FOR ACCEPTING ME JUST AS I AM, SO THAT I CAN BECOME WHAT YOU HAVE CREATED ME TO BECOME."

AMEN.

Chapter Three:

'THE MEANING OF WATER BAPTISM:'

Acts 2:38; KJV. *'Peter said to them, repent and be baptised every one of you in the name of the Lord Jesus Christ for the remission of your sin.'*

The very first thing required of a believer is the personal act of repentance, to have another mind, to change one's mind, to move in the opposite direction by an act of your free will. Peter addressed the Jews in such a way that they would have understood the implication of the words 'repent' and 'baptise.'

It is a command of God.

Acts. 17:30b; KJV. *'All men everywhere to repent.'*

It is a part of the Lord's personal commission to his disciples.

Luke. 26:17; KJV. *'And that repentance and remission of sins should be preached in His name.'*

It is God's desire for all.

2 Peter 3:9; KJV. *'Not willing that any should perish, but that all should come to repentance.'*

Before the act of Baptism there is the requirement for the sinner to repent.

This is not an option but a requirement throughout Scripture, in both the Old and New Testaments.

The remission of your personal sins is by God's Grace toward you the sinner, and can only be given upon the repentance of those sins, by the sinner.

There are two basic phases to a full and genuine act of personal repentance:

1: We all need to accept our personal, sinful state.

Romans 3:23; KJV. *'All have sinned and come short of the glory of God.'*

2: He will honour His Word of restoration.

1 John 1:9; KJV. *'If we confess our sins, He is faithful and just to forgive us our sins, and to cleanse us from all unrighteousness.'*

When it comes to the Baptism, we see that for the people to whom Peter addressed his remarks, he urged them to turn their backs, so to speak, upon Judaism and the fellowship of and relationship with their national identity.

Confession of sin in its collective form, and where necessary its specific form, as that which is affecting, the individual sinner is of paramount importance. There are no exceptions.

It allows God's Grace to become a reality and therefore, Water Baptism is the public evidence of the conversion from sinner to saint.

* WE MOVE FROM THE OLD HUMAN NATURE TO THE NEW SPIRITUAL NATURE IN CHRIST JESUS.'

There is a wonderful parable which has had and continues to have a significant influence upon my life. It is the parable of the Prodigal Son.

Luke 15:11-32; NLT. *'To illustrate the point further, Jesus told them this story: 'A man had two sons. The younger son told his father, 'I want my share of your estate now, before you die.' So, his father agreed to divide his wealth between his sons.*

A few days later this younger son packed all his belongings and moved to a distant land, and there he wasted all his money in wild living. About the time his money ran out, a great famine swept over the land, and he began to starve. He persuaded a local farmer to hire him, and the man sent him into his fields to feed the pigs. The young man became so hungry that even the pods he was feeding the pigs looked good to him. But no one gave him anything.

When he finally came to his senses, he said to himself, 'At home even the hired servants have food enough to spare, and here I am dying of hunger! I will go home to my father and say, Father, I have sinned against both heaven and you, and I am no longer worthy of being called your son. Please take me on as a hired servant.

So, he returned home to his father. And while he was still a long way off, his father saw him coming. Filled with love and compassion, he ran to his son, embraced him, and kissed him.

His son said to him, 'Father, I have sinned against both heaven and you, and I am no longer worthy of being called your son.'

But his father said to the servants, 'Quick! Bring the finest robe in the house and put it on him. Get a ring for his finger and sandals for his feet. And kill the calf we have been fattening.

We must celebrate with a feast, for this son of mine was dead and has now returned to life. He was lost, but now he is found.'

*REJECTION OF AND A DELIBERATE DECISION TO TURN AWAY FROM A SINFUL LIFE.

Luke 15:18-19; KJV. *'I will arise and go to my father, and I will say to him, father I have sinned against heaven and before you. I am no more worthy to be called your son. Make me therefore as one of your hired servants.'*

The eternal promise from an eternal God, is of Identification of the Real Relationship between God, our Creator, and Mankind the created in Everlasting Fellowship.

Romans 6:4-5; KJV. *'Therefore, we are buried with Him by baptism into death that like as Christ was raised up from the dead by the glory of the Father; even so we also should walk in newness of life. For if we have been planted together in the likeness of His death, we shall be also in the likeness of his Resurrection.'*

Baptise means literally to be dipped. The Greek word, 'Baptizo' is to dip, signifying the dying of a garment. We also could use the word to define immersion and submersion, of one object into another.

For the Christian, the word baptise means, to totally submit ourselves to God's perfect and divine will, to be therefore, literally buried as Christ Jesus was, so that God can do with us the same as He has done in Christ Jesus our Lord.

Christian 'water baptism' can only come after the acknowledgement of personal sin. This is then followed by our obedience to the command of Jesus to be identified through death, burial, and the resurrection with Him.

Baptism then is seen to be in three parts:

    1. We are buried under the water just as Christ was buried in the tomb.

    2. We are raised up from the waters of baptism just like Christ was raised up by the glory of the father.

    3. We can walk in a new life of victory just as Christ our Lord and Saviour does, in obedience to the Father's will.

The requirement of faith in the principle of Baptism, needs for the sinner to understand, at least, the faith, which is declared.

    Colossians 2:12-15; NLT. *'For you were buried with Christ when you were baptised. And with him you were raised to new life because you trusted the mighty power of God, who raised Christ from the dead.*

You were dead because of your sins and because your sinful nature was not yet cut away. Then God made you alive with Christ, for he forgave all our sins.

He cancelled the record of the charges against us and took it away by nailing it to the cross. In this way, he disarmed the spiritual rulers and authorities. He shamed them publicly by his victory over them on the cross.'

Ten things to remember about the Old Testament story of Noah and the ark found in chapters 6-8 of Genesis.

1: It was not the water that saved Noah and his family, it was the ark, an Old Testament type of Christ.

2: Baptism in water does not save the soul. Faith in the death, burial, and the Resurrection of Jesus, of which baptism signifies, does however, save the soul, through a personal identification with him.

3: Noah and his family were brought into a new and clean world by the washing over of the water.

4: We also are given a new, a clean, and a fresh start in life by the washing of the waters of baptism.

5: This baptism symbolises the security in the same spirit that raised up Christ from the dead, and He dwells in us because of this very truth. Our attitude towards this, our need to be baptised, is very important.

Acts 2:41; KJV. *'Gladly received his word and were baptised.'*

6: Every believer should be baptised. However, there are exceptions that once more gives us reason to know 'Our God of Common-sense.' *This is the title of my second book.*

Death after conversion, but which occurs before a place and time of Water Baptism can be arranged, does not take away our repentance, nor deny God's promise of our eternal destiny with Jesus.

7: Baptism signifies our obedience to the command of God and our faithfulness in following Christ's example in a symbolic manner.

It is a mark of the public resolve to live according to how Jesus lived and therefore the acceptance of living life God's way rather than our own.

8: Baptizo – to be thoroughly immersed, means, to personally get rid of the stinking thinking of our old self, and be infilled with the totality of God and his word. in the new creation reality of 'Living the New Life in Jesus.'

9: Because baptism follows repentance, the word of God tells us that infants and babies, who because of their inability to comprehend the meaning of sin, cannot be baptised.

However, they can and should be dedicated to Him, just as Jesus was dedicated as a baby:

Luke 2:21-23; NLT. *'Eight days later, when the baby was circumcised, he was named Jesus, the name given him, by the angel, even before he was conceived. Then it was time for their purification offering, as required by the law of Moses after the birth of a child; so, his parents took him to Jerusalem to present him to the Lord.*

The law of the Lord says, 'If a woman's first child is a boy, he must be dedicated to the LORD.'

10: Baptism in water signifies the death of the old life and the putting on of the new life by our identification with Christ.

*'TO ACKNOWLEDGE JESUS AS MY SAVIOUR
IS BASED ON GOD'S GRACE;
TO ACKNOWLEDGE JESUS AS MY LORD
IS BASED ON MY COMMITMENT AND OBEDIENCE
TO HIS WORD.'*

Chapter Four:
'ENABLING OF THE HOLY SPIRIT IN POWER.'

Acts 1:5; KJV. *'For John truly baptised with water, but you shall be baptised with the Holy Spirit not many days hence.'*

A: The baptism performed by John, was recognised as valid by Jesus. Jesus himself needed to undergo the ministrations of John the Baptist so that 'all Scripture might be fulfilled.'

B: The baptism in the Spirit however was a promise in both the Old Testament, and brought to fruition in the New Testament, when it was received by the disciples gathered in the upper room.

C: Jesus clearly points out that; Believing on Him, as Lord and Saviour are different than that of being baptised in the Holy Spirit.

D: IT IS NOT TRUE ... that we are not saved unless we speak in tongues.

As we have discovered in the first chapter Salvation: An Eternal Life Experience', that it is according to the Scriptures; Romans 10:9-10; that we are saved.

Romans 10:9-13; NLT. *'If you openly declare that Jesus is Lord and believe in your heart that God raised him from the dead, you will be saved. For it is by believing in your heart that you are made right with God, and it is by openly declaring your faith that you are saved.*

As the Scriptures tell us, "Anyone who trusts in him will never be disgraced. "Jew and Gentile are the same in this respect. They have the same Lord, who gives generously to all who call on him. For everyone who calls on the name of the LORD will be saved.'

In Chapter One, we have already established that the Greek word Exousia means authority, and that this is the Authority through which we can call ourselves Kings Kids (or as I like to say H.R.H.s).

Likewise, we established the second meaning for the English word, power. The word Power has its root in the Greek word Dunamis which means ability, from which we get the understanding of dynamic or dynamite.

Acts 1:8; KJV. *'But you shall receive power after, the Holy Spirit has come upon you, and you shall be witnesses of Me in Jerusalem, in all Judea and in Samaria, even unto the uttermost parts of the earth.'*

This ability, or Dunamis power, is given to us by God through the baptism of the Holy Spirit. It is the same release of power that is promised to the believers in the upper room.

This was when Jesus promised to send them another, the Comforter and Enabler, when He returned to the Father.

John 16:7; KJV. *'Nevertheless, I tell you the truth; It is expedient for you that I go away: for if I go not away, the Comforter will not come unto you; but if I depart, I will send him unto you.'*

The Holy Spirit is known as the Comforter. It means to be called to the side of, or to comfort, to help and counsel.

What a wonderful, thoughtful, and caring God we have. He, who looks after our every need, Jesus knew that He would have to go up, to be with his Father, so that He could then send the Comforter down to us.

He knew our need and met it fully, through the Holy Spirit, who is the Enabler of our ministry in Christ Jesus.

    1: The Bible tells us that to every believer is given the ministry of reconciliation.

    2Corinthians 5:18; KJV. *'And all things [are] of God, who has reconciled us to himself by Jesus Christ, and has given to us the ministry of reconciliation;'*

This means that by our believing faith and therefore our right standing with God through Jesus, we are given, each one of us who believes, the special ministry of reconciliation.

It is for this reason, this purpose, which God has sent to us His Holy Spirit. It is the Enabling power of the Holy Spirit that, working through our lives, gives us the strength and wisdom, knowledge and faith, miracles and healing, ability to communicate with the heavenly language and interpret (that which is the gift rather than the utterance), with prophecy and revelation and with the discerning of Spirit.

It is of great importance that we understand that all of these 'gifts' are for our use as we witness the Glory and Presence of God, and we can do this, through our personal testimony, of The GOOD NEWS of our Christianity.

There is a chorus which I have had in my heart to share with you:

'It's such Good News:'
Its such good news that Jesus loves me.
He came and died that we might live.
My heart rejoices I'm singing Glory!
Its such good news that Jesus lives.'

Katherine Thorton

Acts 2:4; KJV. *'And they were all filled with the Holy Spirit and began to speak in other tongues, as the Spirit gave them utterance.'*

It is important to remember that a witness is a person with firsthand knowledge or experience. And that we as believers recognise that:

* HE IS: OUR SAVIOUR-LORD-BAPTISER-HEALER, AND COMING KING.

2: For us to realise the potential within us, we must become active participants in the witnessing program. This is a powerful weapon against Satan because the witness is in the Power of His Resurrection.

3: There is no room in the believer's heart for timidity.

2Timothy 1:6-11; NLT *'And I know that same faith continues strong in you. This is why I remind you to fan into flames the spiritual gift God gave you when I laid my hands on you. For God has not given us a spirit of fear and timidity, but of power, love, and self-discipline. So, never be ashamed to tell others about our Lord. And do not be ashamed of me, either even though I'm in prison for him.*

With the strength God gives you, be ready to suffer with me for the sake of the Good News.

For God saved us and called us to live a holy life. He did this, not because we deserved it, but because that was his plan from before the beginning of time—to show us his grace through Christ Jesus.

And now he has made all this plain to us by the appearing of Christ Jesus, our Saviour. He broke the power of death and illuminated the way to life and immortality through the Good News.' I Am,

Every one of the believers assembled in the upper room, as the Lord had instructed them, were filled with the Holy Spirit and they all spoke in tongues.

Acts 2:1-8; NLT. *'On the day of Pentecost all the believers were meeting together in one place. Suddenly, there was a sound from heaven like the roaring of a mighty windstorm, and it filled the house where they were sitting.*

Then, what looked like flames or tongues of fire appeared and settled on each of them. And everyone present was filled with the Holy Spirit and began speaking in other languages, as the Holy Spirit gave them this ability.

At that time there were devout Jews from every nation living in Jerusalem. When they heard the loud noise, everyone came running, and they were bewildered to hear their own languages being spoken by the believers.

They were completely amazed. "How can this be?" they exclaimed. These people are all from Galilee, and yet we hear them speaking in our own native languages!

33

about the wonderful things God has done!" They stood there amazed and perplexed. "What can this mean?" they asked each other.'

4: Scripture tells of three identifiable indicators associated with what occurred that day, from the upper room experience.

A: The evidence was audible: (that something different was occurring) The 'Sound (as of) a mighty rushing wind.'

B: It was Visible: 'Tongues (as of) fire.' The expression – 'as of' in the above two indicators, could be understood to present to the reader 'it sounded like' and 'it looked like.' Respectively.

C: The third was speaking in other tongues (other than their native or known), which evidenced the presence of the Holy Spirit.

Although they, the disciples, did the actual speaking, it was the Holy Spirit who gave them the ability of expression – channel to God – so to speak.

The Holy Spirit is the direct communicator between God and the believer, and the believer and God.

5: Witnessed the presence of the Holy Spirit.

Acts 10:44-47; N LT. *'While Peter spoke these words, the Holy Ghost fell on all of them which heard the word. And they of the circumcision which believed were astonished, as many as came with Peter, because that on the Gentiles also was poured out the gift of the Holy Ghost. For they heard them speak with tongues and magnify God.*

Then answered Peter, 'Can any man forbid water, that these should not be baptised, which have received the Holy Ghost as well as we?'

The above passage reveals to us the power of the witness of the Holy Spirit as is evidenced by speaking in tongues, irrespective of race colour or culture.

It also tells us that there are many who are filled with the Holy Spirit before they are Baptised in water.

However, there is a warning against error.

Speaking in tongues, as described in the above passages of scripture, does not indicate that the speaking, audible act of sound, is the power. It is merely evidence of the power resident, in all believers.

6: 'Natural Progression' in the lives of the early disciples, and then the many other believers who have followed throughout the time of the New Testament, are 'Indicative of God's Grace', as dispensed to those who would accept a renewed life with Him, through Jesus Christ the Saviour, of all who, would believe and follow with, 'The armour of God's anointing – 'The Way, the Truth, and the Life,' as promised throughout Gods word. *This subject is expanded in my Book by that Title, released in May 2024.*

Acts 2:38; KJV. *'Then Peter said unto them, Repent, and be baptised every one of you in the name of Jesus Christ for the remission of sins, and you shall receive the gift of the Holy Spirit.'*

It is clear from this and many other Scriptures that the Baptism in the Holy Spirit is always preceded by repentance from our dead and sinful lifestyle.

It is just as clear that, although in this instance, water baptism is stated as an aspect of the progression, the Holy Spirit Baptism does not necessarily depend upon Water Baptism, but it does depend upon Salvation.

7: The Gift is Not Rubbish.

Matthew 7:9-12; NLT. *'You parents—if your children ask for a loaf of bread, do you give them a stone instead? Or if they ask for a fish, do you give them a snake? Of course not! So, if your sinful people know how to give good gifts to your children, how much more will your heavenly Father give good gifts to those who ask him.' Do to others whatever you would like them to do to you. This is the essence of all that is taught in the law and the prophets.'*

This new language is not some Mumbo Jumbo, but it is the heavenly language given by our Heavenly Father through the Holy Spirit so that we, in our spirit, may directly have communication with Him.

This language however is always under our control and is functioned or operated by our own free will. This wonderful God of ours is hereby enabling us to determine the level of our relationship with Him. This is perhaps the greatest mystery of all. Why would such a powerful Creator God as this leave Himself open to rejection by such mere mortals as you and me? The answer is that for those of Faith it is clear and for those without Faith is never will be.

8: God Never Lets Us Down.

Acts 2:39; KJV. *'For the promise is unto you, and to your children, and to all that are afar off, [even] as many as the Lord our God shall call.'*

This is first and foremost a promise of God. This promise is God's Word to all believers and therefore He is not able to break it. We have a supreme, absolute guarantee which has been sealed, never to be broken. It is worth repeating:

'GOD CANNOT BREAK HIS WORD,
HE NEVER FAILS – HE DOES NOT LIE.
WHEN WE SAY YES TO JESUS, GOD SAYS YES TO US!

When we receive the Baptism of the Holy Spirit, we also receive the power, ability to effectively witness. This witness is powerful because of our personal testimony of what the Lord God has done, for us, by the power of the Holy Spirit, Whom He said He would send to comfort and enable us.

Such a witness is neither sermonising nor of Bible bashing zeal. It is a simple telling of the truth revealed by the Holy Spirit within us. This is the truth of Christ Jesus the Son of the Living God, who is Glorified, Risen and Ascended,

When we receive the Baptism of the Holy Spirit, we can rejoice in a new freedom of expression. This newfound expression of joy is the same as that experienced by the disciples whom we read about in the New Testament.

This new language is not only evidence of the Holy Spirit at work within us, the believer, but also an expression of our love and wonderment of the works and presence of the Living God.

The Holy Spirit is available to all believers of all ages, irrespective of age, race, colour and or Christian denomination. The only prerequisite is that one should believe in Jesus Christ the Risen Saviour and have an absolute acceptance of Him and His Word, (they are one) freely expressed.

The following are other incidences where speaking in tongues is seen, or should I say heard, as evidence of the Baptism of the Holy Spirit. It is sometimes accompanied by other evidence and sometimes standing alone as (the) evidence of the baptism.

Acts 2:4; KJV. *'And they were all filled with the Holy Ghost, and began to speak with other tongues, as the Spirit gave them utterance.'*

Acts 4:31; KJV. *'And when they had prayed, the place was shaken where they were assembled together; and they were all filled with the Holy Ghost, and they spoke the word of God with boldness.'*

Acts 10:46; KJV. *'For they heard them speak with tongues and magnify God. Then answered Peter.'*

Acts 19:6; KJV. *'And when Paul had laid [his] hands upon them, the Holy Ghost came on them; and they spoke with tongues and prophesied.'*

* *'WHEN WE SAY YES TO JESUS, GOD SAYS YES TO US, THROUGH OUR BELIEVING FAITH.'*

God as The Giver of Good Gifts.

Matthew 7:11; KJV. *'If you then, being evil, know how to give good gifts unto your children, how much more shall your Father which is in heaven give good things to them that ask Him?'*

God Gave Us His Only Begotten Son, Jesus.

John 3:16; KJV. *'For God so loved the world that he gave his only begotten Son, that whosoever believes in him should not perish, but have everlasting life.'*

God is The Giver of Eternal Life.

Romans 6:23; KJV. *'For the wages of sin [is] death; but the gift of God [is] eternal life through Jesus Christ our Lord.'*

Jesus Freely Gave Up His Own Life.

John 10:18; KJV. *'No man takes it from me, but I lay it down of myself. I have power to lay it down, and I have power to take it again. This commandment have I received of my Father.'*

Jesus is the giver of the Holy Spirit: The Comforter and Enabler.

Acts 2:38; KJV. *'Then Peter said unto them, Repent, and be baptised every one of you in the name of Jesus Christ for the remission of sins, and you shall receive the gift of the Holy Ghost.'*

Jesus is the Giver of the Ministry Gifts.

Ephesians 4:8&11; KJV. *'Wherefore he said, when he ascended on high, he led captivity captive and gave gifts unto men. And he gave some, apostles; and some, prophets; and some, evangelists; and some, pastors; and teachers;'*

The Holy Spirit as the Giver of Power Dunamis.

Acts 1:8; KJV. *'But ye shall receive power, after that the Holy Ghost is come upon you: and you shall be witnesses unto me both in Jerusalem, and in all Judea, and in Samaria, and unto the uttermost part of the earth.'*

The Giver of The Fruits of The Spirit.

Galatians 5:22; KJV. *'But the fruit of the Spirit is love, joy, peace, long-suffering, gentleness, goodness, faith, meekness, temperance: against such there is no law.'*

1: **Love:** this type of love is agape unconditional and everlasting.

2: **Joy:** that condition of the mind and heart which is confident that he who has begun a good work in you the believer is enabled to see the good in all things which God has purposed.

3: **Peace:** we exercise a tranquillity because the believer has a confidence in him and his word.

4: **Long-suffering:** allows the enabling of and the maintenance of calmness during a storm because the believer sees and stands on the promises of God and his Word.

5: **Gentleness:** bringing empathy and understanding to those who are hurting.

6: **Goodness:** reaching out to those, who have no hope, with tenderness and softness – in spirit and in behaviour.

7: **Faith:** when all hope is gone the is when the fruitfulness of the believer's faith is of paramount importance.

8: **Meekness;** strength under control, is that fruit, when emotions run away, so to speak, the believer can exercise objectivity, strength, and control

9: **Temperance:** moderation in all things, allowing the believer to have ultimate control of self under all circumstances.

Chapter 5:
INTRODUCTION TO THE SPIRITUAL GIFTS:

1 Corinthians 12:1-11; NLT. *'Now, dear brothers and sisters, regarding your question about the special abilities the Spirit gives us. I do not want you to misunderstand this.*

You know that when you were still pagans, you were led astray and swept along in worshipping speechless idols. So, I want you to know that no one speaking by the Spirit of God will curse Jesus, and no one can say Jesus is Lord, except by the Holy Spirit.

There are different kinds of spiritual gifts, but the same Spirit is the source of them all. There are different kinds of service, but we serve the same Lord. God works in different ways, but it is the same God who does the work in all of us.

A spiritual gift is given to each of us so we can help each other.

To one person the Spirit gives the ability to give wise advice;

To another the same Spirit gives a message of special knowledge.

The same Spirit gives great faith to another,

And to someone else the one Spirit gives the gift of healing.

He gives one person the power to perform miracles, and another the ability to prophesy.

He gives someone else the ability to discern whether a message is from the Spirit of God, or from another spirit.

Still another person is given the ability to speak in unknown languages,

While another is given the ability to interpret what is being said. It is the one and only Spirit who distributes all these gifts. He alone decides which gift each person should have.'

It is the Holy Spirit who distributes all these gifts. He alone decides which of these gifts each person should have and when they should use them – always to the Glory of God.

*GOD CANNOT STOP GIVING TO THOSE WHO WOULD USE HIS GIFT, ACCORDING TO HIS WILL.

It is one of the principles of God, through which His love is always expressed. His ability to give is passed on to us through the impartation of His nature, and so it surely follows, that He looks for this same quality in those, not only whom He loves, but in those who confess their love for Him.

Within the Church worldwide there is a quickening of the Spirit. The refreshing of the things of God is pouring out through the revival of the Spiritual Gifts and as a result there are Eight Questions which need answering;

1. What are the Gifts?
2. Why have they not been used in the last period?
3. What right do we have using them today?
4. How can we use them safely?
5. When can we use them and with whom?
6. Will we lose control if we let these gifts loose?
7. What are the safeguards if any?
8. Is it dangerous to use them if you do not know how/why?

There are many other questions, too many to discuss at this place and time. All we can say is that it is a real move given under the anointing of God through the Holy Spirit, causing many peoples of the world to be blessed and brought close to Him who is the Giver of Life Eternal.

There is a life and vitality which has not been witnessed for perhaps many centuries taking place bringing with it a revitalisation of the Christian community. Not only as a worldwide body of believers but also in the denominational and local sense. Praise the Lord.

The Apostle Paul writes three chapters of his letter to the Corinthian church concerning the subject of the Gifts of the Spirit and the issue of speaking in other tongues.

We understand from the general tone of his letter and from the history of the early church that the Corinthian believers were having some problems in handling this whole concept. One of the reasons for this was their distinct lack of teaching upon the matter. It was to this end that Paul addressed himself.

In the twelfth chapter Paul gives what can only be described as a general overview of the Gifts, and explains the identifying factors which may accompany – be present – as evidential indicators of the Holy Spirit.

It is unfortunate that in some cases, there has been, what we might term a 'stumbling block' to many people, the ability to speak in a language not known to the orator.

However, we can see the enemy at work, in the same way as he did in the Garden of Eden, when he – by innuendo – deceived Eve with the Apple, so to speak.

In the thirteenth chapter Paul exhorts the Corinthian Church to use the gifts of the Holy Spirit, in an attitude of love.

In the fourteenth chapter Paul majors on the operation of the three voice gifts, Tongues, Interpretation and Prophecy

So let us take them in the order in which Paul addressed the Corinthians. After all, in this the 21st century, it is not beyond us, to be considered, in many ways, just like the Corinthians, in our selfishness and pride.

How can we be sure that what we do is a part of what God wants for us? How can we be sure that what we do is genuine and really from God and not from Satan?

1 Corinthians 12:1; KJV. *'Now concerning spiritual [gifts], brethren, I would not have you ignorant.'*

The first thing to notice is that Paul recognises that the problem was not in a deliberate abuse of the Gifts of the Holy Spirit, but rather, in the ignorance with which the Corinthians attempted to use them.

The Gifts, which were manifest, were both genuine and true in the sense that yes, they were from God and yes, they could be used by the believers.

What was not understood was the way such Gifting were to be used. An attitude of heart was needed that would bring blessing to the receiver and Glory to the Giver of the Gifts, God.

The Corinthian believers were overjoyed with the truly charismatic effects which were flowing but got themselves very confused in the process. Paul quickly got to the nub of the problem and exhorted them to consider his advice as a 'Father in the faith.'

This is where the first warning or caution note is sounded, and without guidance it is always possible to go overboard, so to speak, and thereby drown in the very thing which gives us pleasure.

We must always bear in mind that there are two ways to handle a gift.

    A. Receive the Gift and use it, as per the instructions. Note that Paul had already perceived that it was in the main, a lack of teaching that created the problem for the Corinthian Christians

    B. Receive it and ignore – 'I do it my way' – in which case we most probably will wreck or abuse it.

The truth of the charismatic move within the Corinthian church, and in the church of this current time, is that we should always be aware that, but for the Grace of God, we can err and thereby abuse the very Gifts which our Heavenly Father wishes to give us.

It is therefore an *imperative for Christian Growth* that we should *avail ourselves of the Knowledge through sound teaching*, and the *maturity, through consistent application*, so that *we may build* what is after all, *solid protection against the wiles of the devil.*

{Please note the important words which are highlighted in the foregoing sentence, because they will give – to you the reader – the sense of urgency *NEEDED IN THE WORLD IN WHICH WE LIVE]*

There is a 'Test' set before each individual person who accepts Jesus and its worth has been established over the many years by those who have witnessed the veracity of its wisdom and truthfulness.

    1 Corinthians 12:3; NLT. *'Wherefore I give you to understand, that no man speaking by the Spirit of God calls Jesus accursed: and [that] no man can say that Jesus is the Lord, but by the Holy Ghost.'*

Paul gave the Christians in the Corinthian church – as he does for us all in PRESENT TIMES – an infallible test concerning the authenticity of the Spiritual Gifts. We cannot dishonour Jesus Christ, or God, whilst we speak or act under the Authority of the Holy Spirit. Compare this Scripture and test every spirit accordingly, by the Glory test:

    1John4:1-3; NLT. *'Beloved, believe not every spirit, but try the spirits whether they are of God: because many false prophets are gone out into the world. Hereby know you the Spirit of God: Every spirit that confesses that Jesus Christ is come in the flesh is of God: And every spirit that confesses not that Jesus Christ is come in the flesh is not of God: and this is that [spirit] of Antichrist, whereof you have heard that it should come; and even now already is it in the world.'*

The Identity Factor:
    Matthew 16:16; KJV. *'And Simon Peter answered and said, Thou art the Christ, the Son of the living God.'*

It is also true that we are incapable of a genuine confession of Jesus as our personal Lord, without the accompanying evidence of the signs which indicate the presence of the Holy Spirit in our life.

BY THEIR FRUITS THEY SHALL BE ESTABLISHED:

Mark 16:15-18; NLT. *'And then he told them, "Go into all the world and preach the Good News to everyone. Anyone who believes and is baptised will be saved. But anyone who refuses to believe will be condemned. These miraculous signs will accompany those who believe:*

They will cast out demons in my name,
They will speak in new languages.
They will be able to handle snakes with safety,
If they drink anything poisonous, it will not hurt them.
They will be able to place their hands on the sick, and they will be healed.'

Let us be reminded that for the New Testament Christian the signs were to follow the believer and their believing, not go in front, as in the Old Testament.

These Gifts then, are for the true believer in Christ, those who not only accept the gift of Life Eternal, but also accept Him as the Lord of their lives. The essential thing is that the Gifts will always bring Honour and Glory to His Name, the Name above all names.

One of the initial questions is that of our worthiness to receive and operate in and with the Gifts of the Holy Spirit. Let us refer to another Scripture, for this is the only infallible source of truth,

*WITHOUT THE QUESTION, THERE CAN BE NO ANSWER:

Luke 11: 9-13; KJV. *'And I say unto you, Ask, and it shall be given you; seek, and you shall find; knock, and it shall be opened unto you. For every one that asks, receives; and he that seeks, finds; and to him that knocks, it shall be opened.*

If a son shall ask bread of any of you that is a father, will he give him a stone? Or if [he asks] a fish, will he for a fish give him a serpent? Or if he shall ask an egg, will he offer him a scorpion?

If you then, being evil, know how to give good gifts unto your children: how much more shall [your] heavenly Father give the Holy Spirit to them that ask him?'

We can be confident that when we ask God for something which will bring glory to His name, and Blessing to His children, we shall have that for which we ask.

The key to the continuance of the operation of the Gifts of the Spirit flowing through our lives is that we use them, the Gifts, wisely and with a sense of responsibility.

Those who have worked with me in the past will know that I am constantly reminding the reader that, personal responsibility, and accountability, go hand in hand. We can be confident therefore, in two things.

When we ask God for a Gift, He will give it, and that He will hold us accountable, because we use it.

If we constantly are in mind of these two conditions, giving them our earnest consideration, the devil will not be able to infiltrate into that which we do.

The divine origin of the Gifts of the Spirit:

1 Corinthians 12:4-7; KJV. *'Now there are diversities of gifts, but the same Spirit. And there are differences of administrations, but the same Lord. And there are diversities of operations, but it is the same God which works all in all. But the manifestation of the Spirit is given to every man to profit withal.*

We can be confident that the Gifts are both genuine and sourced from the very throne room of the Godhead because of the above passage of Scripture. Although the Gifts are both varied and multiple, they are all flowing out from the same origin. Paul continues in this great passage to explain the Gifts and their respective function and purpose.

1 Corinthians 12:4; KJV. *'Now there are diversities of gifts, but the same Spirit.'*

One could not ask for a clearer identification than that which is given in this passage. All nine Gifts of the Spirit mentioned in verses 8-11 are directly sourced from the same Holy Spirit of God.

1 Corinthians 12:5; KJV. *'And there are differences of administrations, but the same Lord.*

Jesus is the source of all ministries and in particular the Ephesians 4: ministries, given to the church after His ascension.

Ephesians 4:8 -12; KJV. *"Wherefore he said, when he ascended up on high, he led captivity captive and gave gifts unto men. (Now that he ascended, what is it, but that he also descended first into the lower parts of the earth?*

He that descended is the same also that ascended far above all heavens, that he might fill all things.)

And he gave some, apostles; and some, prophets; and some, evangelists; and some, pastors, and teachers; For the perfecting of the saints, for the work of the ministry, for the edifying of the body of Christ:'

Notice that the ministry gifts were given for a specific purpose and were to function in a particular manner, being naturally divided into three component parts:

1: PERFECTING OF THE SAINTS. Bringing into fullness the personal and collective Spiritual maturity, so that we might be able to carry out the responsibilities of Christian Living.

2: WORK OF THE MINISTRY. God has decreed that our function as believers, is to be ministries of reconciliation. And this we do by the witness of our testimony as to the Love and Grace of God manifested through our daily living.

3: THE TEACHING OF THE BODY OF CHRIST. This is the knowledge laid down through the relationship between God and his people and is set as the measure for all learning and is therefore the template, so to speak, upon which all teaching is imparted.

The most important understanding which must always be central to exercising of all the gifts without exception, is that they will only bring Glory to His name and will be for the receiver not the giver:

1 Corinthians 12:6; KJV. *'And there are diversities of operations, but it is the same God which works all in all.'*

God is in control, and this is perhaps the greatest safeguard which we have. Jesus the Son, and the Holy Spirit the Enabler, always work under the direction of God the Father. Therefore, that which they do is always according to the Father's will, in all things.

1 Corinthians 12:7; KJV. *'But the manifestation of the Spirit is given to every man to profit withal.'*

God gives gifts for the benefit of those who are His children. He is always mindful of our welfare and best interest.

Another safety measure for us is found in:

Philippians 4:13; KJV. *'I can do all things through Christ which strengthens me.'*

In this powerful Scripture God assures us that He will only ever give to us those things which will strengthen us in service – to Him, and for others.

Chapter Six:
THE NINE GIFTS, EXPLAINED.

1. Their Function and Purpose:

There are nine gifts of the Spirit, and their function and purpose are for the enabling of the church to fulfil its mission and its ministry. We must acknowledge that without these gifts and their supernatural empowerment the church would in no way be able to fulfil the purpose to which it has been called.

When the church is operating in the power of the Holy Spirit and His flowing gifts, the church becomes a dynamic and powerful witness to the message of the Gospel of Jesus Christ.

1 Corinthians 12:7-11; NLT. *'A spiritual gift is given to each of us so we can help each other.*

To one person the Spirit gives the ability to give wise advice;

To another the same Spirit gives a message of special knowledge.

The same Spirit gives great faith to another,

To someone else the one Spirit gives the gift of healing.

He gives one person the power to perform miracles,

To another the ability to prophesy.

He gives someone else the ability to discern whether a message is from the Spirit of God or from another spirit.

Still another person is given the ability to speak in unknown languages,

While another is given the ability to interpret what is being said.'

**IT IS THE ONE SPIRIT
WHO DISTRIBUTES ALL THESE GIFTS.
HE ALONE DECIDES WHICH OF THE GIFTS
EACH BELIEVER SHOULD HAVE.*

The nine gifts are divided into three groups:
1: REVELATION. 2: POWER 3: VERBAL.

And each group has three components.

1.THE GIFTS OF REVELATION.

A. THE WORD OF WISDOM.

The first thing to recognise is that this is not natural wisdom – that which we gain through our worldly pursuits – but it is a portion of the supernatural wisdom which comes from the throne room of the Godhead.

This Spirit empowered wisdom is given to the spirit-filled believer to meet a specific need and for a specific time. It should not be seen as the whole wisdom of God, because were that to be so, it would blow our cotton-picking minds, so to speak.

It may come into our thoughts as just a word or a Scripture which is quickened to us for a given purpose. What we can be sure of is that the Holy Spirit will meet our every need and will be there when we call upon Him in the Name of the Lord.

B. THE WORD OF KNOWLEDGE.

Again, this is not the natural human knowledge gained from books and the like. It is that supernatural knowledge endowed by God and is given as assistance to the ministry of the Word.

It is that which becomes a 'You know, because you know, because you know.' From this knowing comes the acceptance through faith, and it is acted upon without any natural impartation.

The believer acts upon such a word in faith and sees its blessed effectiveness, in the lives of those to whom it is ministered, in confidence and personal assurance. This enables the Christian believer to expand the circumference and the quality of their personal witness, and all in the name of the Lord Jesus and to the glory of God.

C. THE DISCERNING OF SPIRITS.

When dealing with questions related to this Gift, we need to realise that this Gift is not "general" as in the discernment one may have about a particular style in clothing or cosmetics, but it is to do specifically with the discerning of spirits – knowing your enemy – that is required in the deliverance or casting out of evil spirits.

This occurs as a revelation of the presence of evil spirits and their influence within the lives of a person. It can also reveal the number and the nature of such evil spirits.

One other thing for which this Gift is useful, is in the revelation of the weaknesses of those evil forces and how best to deliver them.

The Word tells us that there is a need for much prayer and fasting when encountering such evil forces, and it is suggested therefore, that the most effective way in utilising this Gift is in the same manner, by much prayer and fasting.

Matthew 17:21; KJV. *'Howbeit this kind only goes out by prayer and fasting.'*

Mark 9:29; KJV. *'And He said unto them, 'This kind can come forth by nothing, but by prayer and fasting.'*

2. THE GIFTS OF POWER.

There is the constant interlacing of the Gifts of Faith, Healing, and the Working of Miracles. Nevertheless, because Gods' Word has placed each of them as a separate gifting, then we need to look at them, in the same way.

A. GIFT OF FAITH.

When we believe in God as the Creator and in His Son Jesus Christ as our Saviour and Lord, we require faith. This is however, not the Gift of Faith.

This gift of Faith, is for special occasions and for specific things.

We need to operate this Gift when we are about to launch into a project which we have received through a vision of the Lord.

Some extra capacity which is far above and beyond the natural faith that all have, in the general meaning of the word.

We will need to use this when believing for some supernatural intervention in the affairs of mankind or even in nature itself. In other words when you believe for some special miracle the Gift of Faith is an imperative.

B: THE GIFT OF HEALING,

As in all the other Gifting, is not the general healing ministry which occurs in the Body of believers. This Gift is used when there is the requirement for an intense and concentrated application of faith to believe for God to intercede in the infirmity of man.

God requires of us a special degree of Faith, mixed with a special degree of Authority which only comes from Him, when we exercise this Gift.

Let me give another word of caution here. There is not the slightest doubt in my mind that God in His infinite Wisdom and Grace gives certain people certain ministries. This is also true of the Gifts of the Spirit.

Nevertheless, I believe that it would be incorrect to use a particular label as Healer, Faith Man, Deliverer, etc; when referring to a believer's particular ministry or ability. The danger is that if we allow people, well intentioned that they may be, to put a particular label on us, or indeed themselves, we have the propensity to either defuse or usurp the Authority and Glory, which of course, rightly belongs to Him alone.

**I BELIEVE THAT GOD IS THE AUTHOR, AND MAN IS THE SERVANT OF GOD. WHEN WE SERVE, WE DO SO, IN THE NAME OF HIM, WHOM WE SERVE.*

C. WORKING OF MIRACLES.

This, in its most simple context, means outstanding works of power which are beyond the capacity of mankind to either do, or imagine doing, in the natural sphere of human involvement. We see, in the ministry of Jesus, such miracles.

The first of the 'Jesus' miracles: Turning the water into wine,

John 2:2-11; NLT. *'And Jesus and his disciples were also invited to the celebration. The wine supply ran out during the festivities, so Jesus' mother told him, 'They have no more wine.'*

Dear woman, that is not our problem, Jesus replied. 'My time has not yet come.' But his mother told the servants, 'Do whatever he tells you.'

Standing nearby were six stone water jars, used for Jewish ceremonial washing. Each could hold twenty to thirty gallons. Jesus told the servants, 'Fill the jars with water.' When the jars had been filled, he said, 'Now dip some out, and take it to the master of ceremonies.' So, the servants followed his instructions.

When the master of ceremonies tasted the water that was now wine, not knowing where it had come from (though, of course, the servants knew), he called the bridegroom over. 'A host always serves the best wine first,' he said. 'Then, when everyone has had a lot to drink, he brings out the less expensive wine. But you have kept the best until now!'

This miraculous sign at Cana in Galilee was the first time Jesus revealed his glory. And his disciples believed in him.'

Many miracles which were beyond man's natural understanding, are acknowledged throughout both the Old and New Testaments; For instance, in the Old Testament the miracle of, parting the waters of the Red Sea, so that the people could pass through on dry ground.

Exodus 14:13-18; NLT. *'But Moses told the people, do not be afraid. Just stand still and watch the LORD rescue you today. The Egyptians you see today will never be seen again. The LORD himself will fight for you. Just stay calm.*

Then the LORD said to Moses, 'Why are you crying out to me? Tell the people to get moving!

Pick up your staff and raise your hand over the sea. Divide the water so the Israelites can walk through the middle of the sea on dry ground. And I will harden the hearts of the Egyptians, and they will charge in after the Israelites.

My great glory will be displayed through Pharaoh and his troops, his chariots, and his charioteers. When my glory is displayed through them, all Egypt will see my glory and know that I am the LORD!'

Yet again in the New Testament the stilling of the sea, in a time of storm.

Luke 8:23-25; NLT. *'One day Jesus said to his disciples, 'Let's cross to the other side of the lake.' So, they got into a boat and started out. As they sailed across, Jesus settled down for a nap.*

But soon a fierce storm came down on the lake. The boat was filling with water, and they were in real danger.

The disciples went and woke him up, shouting, 'Master, Master, we're going to drown!'

Then he asked them, 'Where is your faith?' The disciples were terrified and amazed. 'Who is this man?' they asked each other. 'When he gives a command, even the wind and waves obey him!'

Peter walked upon the waters.

Matthew 14:23-32; NLT. *'Immediately after this, Jesus insisted that his disciples get back into the boat and cross to the other side of the lake, while he sent the people home. After sending them home, he went up into the hills by himself to pray. Night fell while he was there alone.*

Meanwhile, the disciples were in trouble far away from land, for a strong wind had risen, and they were fighting heavy waves. About three o'clock in the morning Jesus came toward them, walking on the water.

When the disciples saw him walking on the water, they were terrified. In their fear, they cried out, 'It's a ghost!' But Jesus spoke to them at once. 'Don't be afraid,' he said. 'Take courage. I am here!'

Then Peter called to him, 'Lord, if it's really you, tell me to come to you, walking on the water.'

'Yes, come,' Jesus said. But when he saw the strong wind and the waves, he was terrified and began to sink. 'Save me, Lord!' he shouted. Jesus immediately reached out and grabbed him. 'You have so little faith,' Jesus said. 'Why did you doubt me?'

When they climbed back into the boat, the wind stopped. Then the disciples worshipped him. 'You really are the Son of God!' they exclaimed.'

The feeding of the multitude.

Luke 9:12-17; NLT. *'Late in the afternoon the twelve disciples came to him and said, 'Send the crowds away to the nearby villages and farms, so they can find food and lodging for the night. There is nothing to eat here in this remote place.'*

But Jesus said, 'You feed them.' For there were about 5,000 men there. Jesus replied, 'Tell them to sit down in groups of about fifty each.' So, the people all sat down. Jesus took the five loaves and two fish, looked up toward heaven, and blessed them. Then, breaking the loaves into pieces, he kept giving the bread and fish to the disciples so they could distribute it to the people. They all ate as much as they wanted, and afterwards, the disciples picked up twelve baskets of leftovers!'

Surely the miracles of yesterday are no different than the miracles of today. God is in charge and His will is that we should be a Blessed people.

When we walk along the pathway of life, which He has purposed for us, we can except no less.

**GOD'S ACTS OF LOVE
BECOME OUR MIRACLES OF LIFE,
LIVED OUT FOR HIM.*

3. THE GIFTS OF UTTERANCE.

A. THE GIFT OF TONGUES.

The Gift is an inspired utterance which can only have a meaning, and an understanding, in the Spirit and by the Spirit. It is not to be confused with speaking in tongues, which is the evidence – but not the only one – of the Baptism in the Holy Spirit.

This Gift is not the ability to speak in other known languages but rather it is the ability to speak in a manner which is not understood through the natural knowledge obtained through human learning.

This Gift is only ever recognised as a Godly manifestation when an interpretation is given.

Its specific purpose is to bring an edifying to the believer and to the church. The golden rule applying to this and indeed all the gifts is that such a gift can only bring Comfort, Edification, Exhortation and of course Glory to God, who, after all, has given to us, His gift.

B. THE INTERPRETATION OF TONGUES.

This Gift works in conjunction with the previous Gift of Tongues. It is used by God through the Holy Spirit to bring an understanding to the general believer of that Tongue which they have heard but not understood.

The interpretation has the same specific parameter within which it can operate as all the Gifts. and this is a most valuable gauge, from which to accept or reject that which is spoken.

Such an interpretation must always, and without exception:

COMFORT: What is spoken must bring comfort to the believer.

EDIFICATION: The hearer must be able to apply the message, to their own circumstances.

EXHORTATION: The general thrust must be one of encouragement.

HONOUR TO GOD: This extra component, which is always present, is that of Lifting the Name of Jesus, and bringing Glory to God in the Highest.

When the above is evidenced then there is no need to fear the devil and his trickery, because God has shown through that same evidence, that He is in charge.

C. THE GIFT OF PROPHECY.

As with the other Utterance Gifts this is also an inspired message. It is, as with the Gift of Interpretation given in the known language. Its function is to build up the church and or its members either individually or as a congregation of people.

This Gift is not "preaching a message" which has been prepared for a particular time or place. It is most often a spontaneous word or message given without any prepared agenda. It is also not a Prophetic utterance such as that, which a prophet would utter – but nevertheless a Prophet could also be used by the Holy Spirit to use this particular Gift.

However, there are times when the Gift of Prophecy is given later, when the Holy Spirit has prompted such a message to be given. We can tell whether this is in fact an utterance under the guidance of the Holy Spirit, by the way in which we are spiritually moved to receive it.

Once again, as with the previous Utterance Gifts the guidelines are simple to observe and we will just refer to them as stated under the Gift of Interpretation.

Here are some additional Scriptural references to the use of this Gift:

Laying on of Hands and Prophecy:

1 Timothy 4:14-15; NLT. *'Do not neglect the spiritual gift you received through the prophecy spoken over you when the elders of the church laid their hands on you. Give your complete attention to these matters.'*

The Degree of Faith:

Romans 12:6-8; NLT *'In his grace, God has given us different gifts for doing certain things well. So, if God has given you the ability to prophesy, speak out with as much faith as God has given you:*

If your gift is serving others, serve them well. If you are a teacher, teach well. If your gift is to encourage others, be encouraging. If it is giving, give generously. If God has given you leadership ability, take the responsibility seriously. And if you have a gift for showing kindness to others, do it gladly.'

Prophecy of Future Hope and Encouragement is to be used in the Public (church) Domain:

2Peter 1:19; NLT. *'Because of that experience, we have even greater confidence in the message proclaimed by the prophets. You must pay close attention to what they wrote, for their words are like a lamp shining in a dark place—until the Day dawns, and Christ the Morning Star shines in your hearts.'*

Prophecy is by the Supernatural (Spirit of God).

2Peter 1:20-21; NLT. *'Above all, you must realise that no prophecy in Scripture ever came from the prophet's own understanding, or from human initiative. No, those prophets were moved by the Holy Spirit, and they spoke from God.'*

Prophecy is The Testimony of The Lord.

Revelation 19:10; NLT. *'Then I fell at his feet to worship him, but he said, "No, do not worship me. I am a servant of God, just like you and your brothers and sisters who testify about their faith in Jesus.*

*WORSHIP ONLY GOD.
FOR THE ESSENCE OF PROPHECY
IS TO GIVE A CLEAR WITNESS FOR JESUS.'

Chapter Seven:

'ESTABLISHED IN THE CHURCH.'

1 Corinthians 12: 12-31; KJV. *'For as the body is one, and has many members, and all the members of that one body, being many, are one body: so also, [is] Christ. For by one Spirit are we all baptised into one body, whether [we be] Jews or Gentiles, whether [we be] bond or free; and have been all made to drink into one Spirit.'*

In Australia we had a referendum (Oct 2023) and the people have decided emphatically that we are one people – one nation – drawn together from all over the world, but we are all Australians. Surely this is the human equivalent of the Spiritual application given in this Scripture.

'For the body is not one member, but many. If the foot shall say, because I am not the hand, I am not of the body; is it therefore not of the body? And if the ear shall say, because I am not the eye, I am not of the body; is it therefore not of the body? If the whole body [were] an eye, where [were] the hearing? If the whole [were] hearing, where [were] the smelling?

But now has God set the members every one of them in the body, as it has pleased him. And if they were all one member, where [were] the body?

But now [are they] many members, yet but one body. And the eye cannot say unto the hand, I have no need of you: nor again the head to the feet, I have no need of you. Nay, much more those members of the body, which seem to be, feebler, are necessary:

And those [members] of the body, which we think to be less honourable, upon these we bestow more abundant honour; and our uncomelier [parts] have more abundant comeliness. For our comely [parts] have no needs: but God hath tempered the body together, having given more abundant honour to that [part] which lacked:

That there should be no schism in the body; but [that] the members should have the same care one for another. And whether one member suffers, all the members suffer with it; or one member is honoured, all the members rejoice with it. Now you are the body of Christ, and members.

And God has set some in the church, first apostles, secondarily prophets, thirdly teachers, after that, miracles, then gifts of healing, helps, governments, diversities of tongues. [Are] all apostles? [Are] all prophets? [Are] all teachers? [Are] all workers of miracles? Have all the gifts of healing? Do all speak with tongues? Do all interpret? But covet earnestly the best gifts: and yet I show you a more excellent way.'

What a pity the world could not see the wisdom of the Creator in being 'at one.' Just think of a 'One World' – man and God – in perfect harmony. We can but dream.

{I am in no way implying or advocating a 'One World Government' scenario}.

The false statement that the Gifts were only for the foundational building of the early church, is just one of today's stumbling blocks.

It is the one which we see used within the church rather than by outsiders. The unbeliever does not consider it as an issue, for it has no immediate effect upon them.

But for the Christian the matter is quite different. This is, I suggest, because in embracing the Gifts of the God of Creation as real and relevant for today, we must take on board, so to speak, the responsibility to use those Gifts as the Creator – God – intended.

There becomes an obligation to become Active Christians who are recognised for the testimony of their living epistle standards, and who are committed to see souls won for the Kingdom.

This most assuredly is my personal conviction and motivates me each day in what I do and have faith for the 'Fulfilling my Potential in Christ.' That is why this book is entitled this way.

Mark 16: 17-19; KJV. *'And these signs shall follow them that believe; In my name shall they cast out devils; they shall speak with new tongues; They shall take up serpents; and if they drink any deadly thing, it shall not hurt them; they shall lay hands on the sick, and they shall recover.'*

Note once more that particularly in the New Testament times, the 'signs' follow the believer. What the above passage of Scripture says to me, and I hope to you as well, is:

*WHEN THE BELIEVER BELIEVES, GOD ACTS.

Those Gifts, ordained by God, are placed in the body of Christ as 'weapons of our warfare' and are to assist us in the work of the ministry currently.

Paul explains to the Corinthian believers how to operate the Gifts in a Godly manner.

As the arm, or the foot, or the mouth, or the eyes are set in the body (physical) and are not intended for use other than in conjunction with the rest of the body.

The Gifts are set within the body (Spiritual) and are for the use of the Church members and those to whom God has purposed.

United: We Stand Complete in Him.

1 Corinthians 12:12-13; KJV. *'For as the body is one, and has many members, and all the members of that one body, being many, are one body: so also, [is] Christ. For by one Spirit are we all baptised into one body, whether [we be] Jews or Gentiles, whether [we be] bond or free; and have been all made to drink into one Spirit.'*

The Body of Christ which is commonly called The Church is made up of a much diversified, mixture of humanity. For it to be as effective as is God's design, it needs to have at its centre a unifying factor which can be easily recognised from all the other faiths and ideologies.

A: That Unity Factor is the calling together of Born Again, (by the Spirit of God) believers from all over the world.
B: From every kindred nation, of every colour and from every tribal grouping.

C: From every denomination of the Church, from the individual believer, even to the smallest house meeting.

D: From the established church, to the oldest or the youngest believer, and from the children to the Grandparents amongst us.

God has called us together in His Son Jesus Christ, for fellowship with Him. It sounds too good to be true. Well, it is not only possible but actual in 'Kingdom Living.'

This unity factor is the working in the Holy Spirit, of all that God has made possible for us. He has established it from the beginning, and it has not been taken away. It is this unity in the Spirit which I believe Jesus is referring to in John's Gospel when He describes the alternative functions of the devil and Himself.

John 10:10; KJV. *'The thief comes to steal, and to kill, and to destroy. I am come that they might have life, and that they might have [it] more abundantly.'*

The Holy Spirit functioning in the affairs of the believers, is for every occasion. The Holy Spirit is the unifier, in both an individual and collective sense.

He brings together the Body of Christ. He is the enabler of the Spiritual Gifts. He always acts in the Will of the Father. He is the comforter exhorter, the Paraclete.'

So, we can recognise the various attributes, which flow as a direct positive response to the Scriptures, which God has purposed to give us concerning the Spiritual Gifts.

HOWEVER, IT IS GOD WHO MAKES THE FINAL CALL, WE MUST ALLOW HIS LEADING, FOR THE BEST RESULTS. BECAUSE NOTHING ELSE WILL DO.

The ten principles when the believer is exercising in the Holy Spirit:

1. The spiritual Gifts are given to all believers.
2. The Holy Spirit divides to each believer the Gift, or Gifts, which are needed for their respective use.
3. The Gifts will always bring Glory to the Father, who gave them for that purpose.
4. The Gifts are a service component to the Body of Christ.
5. The Gifts work in unity and in perfect harmony.
6. The Gifts flow automatically and naturally; they don't need to be forced.
7. The believer is in the 'Will of God' when functioning under the power of the Holy Spirit.
8. The Gifts are to be used in the spirit of humility.
9. The believer is always responsible for the presentation of the Gift.
10. The believer will be held accountable to God, because the Gifts were either used or abused.

The wonderful opportunity to serve God within the above 10 principles, speak to me of the challenges that lie before us, in Jesus our Lord.

The oft spoken declared intent of mine is to 'go to church to enjoy all that God has got to give me.' And praise Him in my response. I know that when this happens, I am both a blessing to those with whom I come in contact, and, I am blessed by those I am in fellowship with and of course I am abundantly blessed, of my Father in Heaven.

The Multiplicity of the Believers in Christ:

1 Corinthians 12: 14-17; KJV. *'For the body is not one member, but many.*

If the foot shall say, because I am not the hand, I am not of the body; is it therefore not of the body?

And if the ear shall say, because I am not the eye, I am not of the body; is it therefore not of the body?

If the whole body [were] an eye, where [were] the hearing? If the whole [were] hearing, where [were] the smelling?'

Now tell me. Have you ever seen a head walk down the road without a body? Or have you seen a body walk down the road without its head? – *my church secretary in the Frankston New Life Christian Centre, who was a Sri Lankan, told me that she had witnessed such a thing.* –However, it would be fair to say that most of us have never been confronted with such a scene, I do not think so, because we all know, that we cannot survive or at least be effective, without the coming together in unity, so to speak, as one entity – the whole body, as one.

So, as we referred earlier, the Spiritual Body is treated in the same way as the physical body.

The gifts of God are placed within the Body of Believers for the express purpose, of enhancing the performance of the Body as a whole.

The Body of believers must be unified in the central fact of Jesus Christ as the Saviour of the world, and that He is their individual Saviour due to the personal confession of faith, which has been expressed from within their hearts.

The Gifts however are placed within the Body in such a way as to be a natural extension of the living presence of Jesus in the life of both the personal believer, but also in the church corporate.

God has placed a guiding structure within the life of both the body corporate, but just as importantly, within the heart – spirit – of each believer.

However, the Christian life must not centre around one Gift. For instance:

It is not the Church of Healing, but healing takes place.

> It is not the church of Faith, but faith is present there.

>> It is not the church of miracles, but miracles do happen in the midst of the congregation.

>>> It is not the church of Prophecy, but prophecy is a part of the ongoing ministry of the church of God.

I trust that what has been presented, is both comforting and edifying to your spirit. I further trust that you will be encouraged to extend yourselves in the wonderful realm of 'Kingdom living' as you use the Wonderful Gifts of God through the Holy Spirit.

You can be assured you will never be out of control, never ashamed nor embarrassed, as you extend your ministry gifting.

There are some built in safeguards which God has provided which will protect us from falling.

1. Never one Gift in Domination – They harmonise.

2. Never operative in an unbalanced way – They complement each other.

3. Never is any one Gift self-sufficient – The key function is Inter-dependency.

4. Never is the Gift of God a law unto itself – It is united in Love.

5. Never is the Gift used in discord or rebellion – It is for the building up of the Body of Christ.

Building Blocks of Revival.

1 Corinthians 12:18-25; KJV. *'But now has God set the members every one of them in the body, as it hath pleased him. And if they were all one member, where [were] the body? But now [are they] many members, yet but one body. And the eye cannot say unto the hand, I have no need of you: nor again the head to the feet, I have no need of you.*

No, much more those members of the body, which seem to be feebler, are necessary: And those [members] of the body, which we think to be less honourable, upon these we bestow more abundant honour; and our uncomelier [parts] have more abundant comeliness.

For our comely [parts] have no needs: but God has tempered the body together, having given more abundant honour to that [part] which lacked:'

We are a part of the New Creation, and as such we have been designed to live in the Kingdom. Kingdom living without the use of the Gifts of the Spirit is like a fish out of water, or an eagle without wings.

We are designed to use the Gifts and are ineffective without them. The church – that is you and me, in the collective believer-ship within the Local Body – is in fact, impotent, without the manifestation of the Gifts of the Spirit being evidenced therein.

In fact, we would ourselves a favour, so to speak, by listening to the voice of John Wesley who writes in one of his sermons, 'The More Excellent Way' concerning the abuse (by non-use) of the Holy Spirit Gifts. 'The cause of this was not, as has been vulgarly supposed, because there was no more occasion for them, because all the world were become Christians.

The real cause was, the love of many, almost all Christians, so-called, was waxed cold. The Christians had no more of the Spirit of Christ than the other heathens;

The Son of Man when He came to examine His church could hardly find faith. This was the real cause why the extraordinary gifts of the Holy Spirit were no longer to be found in the Christian church, because the Christians were turned heathen again, and had only a dead form left.'

The freshness and availability of the Gifts of the Holy Spirit are for us today. They have always been ready for our use. The question to be answered is: Are we ready to use them?

This is the challenge; to seek even a better way in which to use the Gifts of the Spirit.

We need to only make ourselves available in service to Him, hear the Voice of the Lord, obey His command, and trust in His ability and exercise His abounding Love to succeed.

Chapter Eight:
'A GREATER GIFT':

1Corinthians 13; NLT. *'If I could speak all the languages of earth and of angels, but did not love others, I would only be a noisy gong or a clanging cymbal. If I had the gift of prophecy, and if I understood all of God's secret plans and possessed all knowledge, and if I had such faith that I could move mountains, but did not love others, I would be nothing. If I gave everything I have to the poor and even sacrificed my body, I could boast about it; but if I did not love others, I would have gained nothing.*

Love is patient and kind. Love is not jealous or boastful or proud or rude. It does not demand its own way. It is not irritable, and it keeps no record of being wronged. It does not rejoice about injustice but rejoices whenever the truth wins out. Love never gives up, never loses faith, is always hopeful, and endures through every circumstance.

Prophecy and speaking in unknown languages and special knowledge will become useless. But love will last forever! Now our knowledge is partial and incomplete, and even the gift of prophecy reveals only part of the whole picture! But when the time of perfection comes, these partial things will become useless.

When I was a child, I spoke and thought and reasoned as a child. But when I grew up, I put away childish things. Now we see things imperfectly, like puzzling reflections in a mirror, but then we will see everything with perfect clarity.

All that I know now is partial and incomplete, but then I will know everything completely, just as God now knows me completely.

Three things will last forever—faith, hope, and love—and the greatest of these is love.'

We should note that where the word 'Charity' appears, it is seen as an emphasis on the word, Agape, 'Selfless Love' not selfish love.

The first thing to observe in this wonderful letter to the Corinthian Church was that Paul encouraged them into a new phase of their Christian living. He was really saying to them the words which have been repeated in song. "What the world needs now is love, sweet love."

The truth of the matter is that it is the church, which needs to define and live out the life of love as exampled by our Lord. A need for kindness, for consideration and understanding and empathy. We know that meekness is in fact an opposite of weakness because:

*MEEKNESS MEANS STRENGTH UNDER CONTROL

Too often – in the western world – that we should exercise an ill thought through sort of compassion we hear that sympathy is the right road, when in fact empathy, would lead to a better understanding.

Indeed, to find our way back to God, can be gauged by our willingness to 'Walk in the Light of God's Word' – but sadly we have lost our way, primarily because we want to do it our way.

It would be better for us to humble ourselves, seeking to establish the only way that can ever be successful and that is;

'GOD'S WAY.'

Selflessness, an Agape relationship, just like the Father, His Son Jesus, and the Holy Spirit had in the beginning. This was the sad situation in that humanity grew away from a loving relationship necessary for God to sacrifice His only Son Jesus. The state of play today, and in this, I also include the Church universal, is one of self-importance, of making one-self, the centre of importance and value.

In the operating of the gifts which God has given to the church, Paul, clearly identifies the stumbling block, the 'State of Play,' so to speak, the barrier through which the church is today finding itself basically impotent. (See the earlier notation from John Wesley.)

As I have been in the habit of writing notes to myself over the years, one such note says this,

*SOME CHRISTIANS HAVE THE CONCEPT
OF SELF-IMPORTANCE
AND THUS, BECOME IMPOTENT
IN THE THINGS THAT REALLY MATTER.'

This is because the church or the individual, tries to make it, or themselves, indispensable, by tending to desire through their own emphasis, the importance of the messenger of the gift, rather than the gift and or the giver, God.

Paul ends chapter 12: with these words: 1 Corinthians 12:31; NLT. *'But covet earnestly the best gifts: and yet show I unto you a more excellent way.'*

The error has frequently been made, in believing that Paul was saying the gifts of the Spirit, were secondary to Love.

However, I believe that he was clearly saying, that, when the gifts, which he had spoken of, were mixed with that selfless, agape love, which comes from the very essence of God Himself, then and only then would God be glorified.

God's love is a controlled love. In fact, there is nothing about God which is not under His Divine control.

Any power which is loose and not under a form of discipline, becomes dangerous and tends to destroy rather than build. It in fact becomes a law unto itself.

Because of this, it is intended that the spiritual gifts are subject to divine laws. To draw a thumb nail sketch of what we have discovered so far would go something like this.

The gifts of God given to the believers, will work through the character of the believer, and is operated in, divine wisdom, love, and power, so that God is glorified by the blessing which He has thus given.

The Old Testament gives us a good understanding of the above, in its description of the robes *of the High Priest.*

    Exodus 39:25; KJV. *'And they made bells [of] pure gold, and put the bells between the pomegranates upon the hem of the robe, round about between the pomegranates;'*

The bells were separated so that each had a distinctive sound yet together held a symphony. This is just like the true operation of the Gifts of the Spirit.

When the individual Gift is in symphony with Love then the world recognises Gods Harmony and can give to Him the Glory and Praise.

Jesus is the High Priest and the bells which He uses, His Gifts in the Father, through the Holy Spirit, indeed does have a harmony as they together work the Works of God.

Jesus our High Priest has given these gifts to the believing church. This is just as true today as it was in the days of Paul and John as it was in the days of Wesley and Luther. Indeed, as it is wherever the people of God obey and come in love and submission to His divine Word.

During the life of the New Testament Church and its ongoing pursuit of excellence in the future direction of both individual and corporate lives, you are encouraged to embrace what is the function and the purpose of the Gifts.

It is at the beginning that we need to have a clear understanding that the Gifts, without love, neither glorify God nor consequently bring life to His people.

When we declare that the motivating force supporting all of God's gifts is in fact L O V E what then, are the Marks of Love, which we find in God's Word?

    1 Corinthians 13:4-7; AMP. *'Love endures long and is patient and kind; love never is envious nor boils over with jealousy, is not boastful or vainglorious, does not display itself haughtily.*

It is not conceited (arrogant and inflated with pride); it is not rude (unmannerly) and does not act unbecomingly.

Love (God's love in us) does not insist on its own rights or its own way, for it is not self-seeking; it is not touchy or fretful or resentful; it takes no account of the evil done to it, [it pays no attention to a suffered wrong]. It does not rejoice at injustice and unrighteousness but rejoices when right and truth prevail.

Love bears up under anything and everything that comes, is ever ready to believe the best of every person, its hopes are fadeless under all circumstances, and it endures everything [without weakening].'

Galatians 5:22-23; KJV. *'But the fruit of the Spirit is love, joy, peace, long-suffering, gentleness, goodness, faith, meekness, temperance: against such there is no law.'*

Perhaps the most important aspect which can be gained from these two Scripture readings is that of the clear balance between the Fruit of the Spirit and the Gifts of the Spirit.

They also illustrate their joint affinity with Love as the life force of their respective relationships both vertical and horizontal. We can rest confident of that when we operate as living Epistles, proclaiming the Good News, by the blending of the Spiritual Gifts:

1 Corinthians 12:13-14; NLT. *'The human body has many parts, but the many parts make up one whole body. So, it is with the body of Christ. Some of us are Jews, some are Gentiles, some are slaves, and some are free.*

But we have all been baptised into one body by one Spirit, and we all share the same Spirit.'

The Fruits of the Spirit found in:

Galatians 5:22; NLT. *'But the Holy Spirit produces this kind of fruit in our lives: love, joy, peace, patience, kindness, goodness, faithfulness, gentleness, and self-control. There is no law against these things!'*

*WE BECOME EFFECTIVE IN OUR WITNESS THROUGH OUR EXERCISING OF THE FRUIT OF THE SPIRIT, THROUGHOUT OUR LIVES AS A LIVING TESTIMONY. IT IS THEN THAT WE HAVE BECOME THIS LIVING EPISTLE.

However, there is a warning contained within the same passages of Scripture. And it is this, we must be constantly on guard against the fruit of the flesh:

Galatians 5:19-21; KJV. *'Now the works of the flesh are manifest, which are [these]; Adultery, fornication, uncleanness, lasciviousness, Idolatry, witchcraft, hatred, variance, emulation, wrath, strife, sedition, heresies, Envying, murders, drunkenness, revelling, and such like: of the which I tell you before, as I have also told [you] in time past, that they which do such things shall not inherit the kingdom of God.'*

We could so easily be deterred from functioning properly, to our God given capacity, because we recognise that we are not perfect.

However, this is just what the devil would want us to believe. When the devil wants us to believe something you can back it in 'like London to a brick' that what we are thinking is not what God wants us to think. This is what I call 'stinking thinking' because it is contrary to the Word of God.

Romans 5:13-19; NLT. *'When Adam sinned, sin entered the world. Adam's sin brought death, so death spread to everyone, for everyone sinned. Yes, people sinned even before the law was given.*

But it was not counted as sin because there was not yet any law to break. Still, everyone died—from the time of Adam to the time of Moses—even those who did not disobey an explicit commandment of God, as Adam did.

Now Adam is a symbol, a representation of Christ, who was yet to come. But there is a great difference between Adam's sin and God's gracious gift.

For the sin of this one man, Adam, brought death to many. But even greater is God's wonderful grace and his gift of forgiveness to many through this other man, Jesus Christ. And the result of God's gracious gift is very different from the result of that one man's sin.

For Adam's sin led to condemnation, but God's gift leads to our being made right with God, even though we are guilty of many sins. For the sin of this one man, Adam, caused death to rule over many. But even greater is God's wonderful grace and his gift of righteousness, for all who receive it will live in triumph over sin and death through this one man, Jesus Christ.

Yes, Adam's one sin brings condemnation for everyone, but Christ's one act of righteousness brings a right relationship with God and new life for everyone.

Because one-person, disobeyed God, many became sinners. But because one other person obeyed God, many will be made righteous.'

2 Corinthians 5:16; NLT. *'We have stopped evaluating others from a human point of view. At one time we thought of Christ merely from a human point of view. How differently we know him now!*

This means that anyone who belongs to Christ has become a new person. The old life is gone; a new life has begun!'

There is no need to struggle, for the battle has already been won, and we have all become like as Christ, who is eternally Victorious, through His death for us on our personal cross. Therefore, it is with confidence that we go on to live lives poured out for Him in service.

That service is greatly assisted by our faithful application of His spiritual Gifts as not only weapons of warfare but also through our personal and collective testimony.

* *'THAT THE WORLD MAY KNOW*
THE LOVE THAT IT SEEKS
IS AVAILABLE THROUGH
CHRIST JESUS OUR LORD.'

When will the gifts cease?

1 Corinthians 13:8-12; KJV. *'Charity never fails but whether [there be] prophecies, they shall fail; whether [there be] tongues, they shall cease; whether [there be] knowledge, it shall vanish away. For we know in part, and we prophesy in part. But when that which is perfect is come, then that which is in part shall be done away.*

When I was a child, I spoke as a child; I understood as a child, I thought as a child: but when I became a man, I put away childish things.

For now, we see through a glass, darkly; but then face to face: now I know in part; but then shall I know even as also I am known.'

The above verses of Scripture have been used over the years to deny the validity of speaking in tongues. The argument is that if tongues were valid in the time of the early church disciples, then it finished with the death of the last of the Kingdom Apostles.

However, upon examination the above verses provide five truths:

Love Is Eternal –
    Prophecies will Fail –
        Tongues will Cease –
            Knowledge will Pass Away –
                Gifts of The Spirit are Controlled.

The question is not, Is the Scripture true? But rather, when will these things take place?

Verses 8 & 9 tell us what is to happen. And Verses 10-12 tell us when these things will happen.

Perhaps it is again important to remind ourselves that:

* *WHEN SOMETHING IS TAKEN OUT OF CONTEXT IT CAN BECOME A PRETEXT FOR ANYTHING.*

The real answer is that when Christ returns for His Church there will then be no need for the Gifts and Ministries which have been so beneficial to the Church of Christ over the past two thousand years.

I am reminded of Wesley's assertion that the Church is impotent without the proper use of the Gifts.

Paul was clearly identifying himself with the use of the Gifts because he said on several occasions that He spoke in Tongues, and he prophesied.

We must therefore conclude that if it was good enough for Paul, who could most certainly be regarded as a man much used of God, then it should be just as valid and useful for us to use, in this present day and time.

The truth is that we cannot succeed in the Great Commission unless we flow in the Authority of our Saviour and the Ability of the Holy Spirit.

     1 Corinthians 13:13; KJV. *'And now abides faith, hope, charity, these three; but the greatest of these [is] charity.'*

Remembering that the word charity means, in this context, Love, we see that all the gifts are precious, but when used in the attitude of Godly love, it brings,

Blessing and Honour and Glory to God, and to those to whom it is given they bring strength and peace and joy and confidence.

So, in conclusion to this chapter let us join with the Apostle Paul and our contemporary John Wesley and say, when we follow love, and desire to use the Gifts of the Spirit in service to our fellow man and worship of our Lord, that this surely is a: 'more excellent way.'

Chapter Nine:

"THE DYNAMICS OF THE VOCAL GIFTS:"

1 Corinthians 14:2-22; NLT. *'Let love be your highest goal! But you should also desire the special abilities the Spirit gives—especially the ability to prophesy. For if you can speak in tongues, you will be talking only to God, since people will not be able to understand you. You will be speaking by the power of the Spirit, but it will all be mysterious.*

But one who prophesies strengthens others, encourages them, and comforts them. A person who speaks in tongues is strengthened personally, but one who speaks a word of prophecy strengthens the entire church.

I wish you could all speak in tongues, but even more I wish you could all prophesy. For prophecy is greater than speaking in tongues, unless someone interprets what you are saying so that the whole church will be strengthened.

Dear brothers and sisters, if I should come to you speaking in an unknown language, how would that help you? But if I bring you a revelation or some special knowledge or prophecy or teaching, that will be helpful.

Even lifeless instruments like the flute or the harp must play the notes clearly, or no one will recognise the melody. And if the bugler does not sound a clear call, how will the soldiers know they are being called to battle?

It is the same for you. If you speak to people in words they do not understand, how will they know what you are saying? You might as well be talking into empty space.

There are many different languages in the world, and every language has meaning. But if I do not understand a language, I will be a foreigner to someone who speaks it, and the one who speaks it will be a foreigner to me.

And the same is true for you. Since you are so eager to have the special abilities the Spirit gives, seek those that will strengthen the whole church.

So, anyone who speaks in tongues should pray also for the ability to interpret what has been said. For if I pray in tongues, my spirit is praying, but I do not understand what I am saying.

Well then, what shall I do? I will pray in the spirit, and I will also pray in words I understand. I will sing in the spirit, and I will also sing in words I understand.

For if you praise God only in the spirit, how can those who do not understand you praise God along with you? How can they join you in giving thanks when they do not understand what you are saying? You will be giving thanks very well, but it will not strengthen the people who hear you.

I thank God that I speak in tongues more than any of you. But in a church meeting I would rather speak five understandable words to help others than ten thousand words in an unknown language.

Dear brothers and sisters do not be childish in your understanding of these things. Be innocent as babies when it comes to evil but be mature in understanding matters of this kind.

It is written in the Scriptures: 'I will speak to my own people through strange languages and through the lips of foreigners. But even then, they will not listen to me, says the LORD.' '

So, you see that speaking in tongues is a sign, not for believers, but for unbelievers. Prophecy, however, is for the benefit of believers, not unbelievers.

Even so, if unbelievers or people who do not understand these things come into your church meeting and hear everyone speaking in an unknown language, they will think you are crazy.

But if all of you are prophesying, and unbelievers or people who do not understand these things come into your meeting, they will be convicted of sin and judged by what you say. As they listen, their secret thoughts will be exposed, and they will fall to their knees and worship God, declaring, 'God is truly here among you.'

Chapter 14 deals almost exclusively with the three vocal gifts, namely Tongues, Interpretation and Prophecy. However, we must understand that Paul is writing to the Corinthian church, in a particular context.

The Corinthian church could be seen as the first 'charismatic' group of Christian believers, after the initial Pentecost experience of those in the Upper Room. There may well have been others, but the Corinthians were certainly very prominent in the use of the Gifts of the Spirit and the vocal or utterance Gifts in particular.

Unfortunately, they were prone to the abuse of those gifts in as much as they were using them often to the exclusion of other gifts, or EVEN the Word, itself.

Paul's letter then, was an attempt to bring correction to these Christian believers, and in doing so Paul has given to the reader of the present day an impression that speaking in tongues was a less desirable gift than the others. This of course is not what Paul was in fact doing as we shall see. Paul was warning against the abuse of, rather than the use of, the utterance gifts.

His desire was to create an understanding of the gifts, particularly the tongues, and in doing so to create a more beneficial outpouring of those gifts, within the congregation of believers.

Verses 1-5; *'Follow after charity, and desire spiritual [gifts], but rather that you may prophesy. For he that speaks in an [unknown] tongue speaks not unto men, but unto God: for no man understands [him]; howbeit in the spirit he speaks mysteries.'*

Paul in this passage of his writings to the Corinthian Church, was clearly indicating that speaking in tongues was not the 'be all,' in consideration of the other gifts. We should understand that he was bringing a perspective to the use of the utterance gifts.

He told them that it was preferable to speak a word of prophecy which could be understood in the native tongue, rather than the utterance of tongues without interpretation.

WHEN PROPHECY IS USED, THE HEARERS ARE DIRECTLY CONFRONTED WITH THE WISDOM AND SPIRITUAL KNOWLEDGE OF THEIR CREATOR GOD. THIS IS BROUGHT ABOUT THROUGH THE INSPIRATION AND ABILITY OF THE HOLY SPIRIT.

TONGUES – V 2; *'For one who speaks in an (unknown) tongue speaks not unto men but unto God, for no one understands or catches his meaning, because in (Holy) Spirit he utters secret truths and hidden things (not obvious to the understanding.)'*

This occurs when a Christian believer needs to bypass the intellect, worldly understanding, and restriction, and enter a personal relationship, full of praise, worship, and prayer which is outside of the believer's normal dimensions.

If you like, it is as if one would break free of the finite compass of the human mind so that one can directly communicate, at an intimate level with the infinite nature of God.

PROPHESYING – V 3-4; *'But he that prophecy speaks unto men [to] edification, and exhortation, and comfort. He that speaks in an [unknown] tongue edifies himself; but he that prophecy edifies the church.*

I would that you all spoke with tongues, but rather that you prophesied: for greater [is] he, than he that speaks with tongues, except he interprets, that the church may receive edifying.'

What is very clear from the writings of Paul and in our personal witness of such operations in the use of the gifts is that there is a great similarity between the interpretation and the prophecy.

It is to this, that Paul is giving clarity. This equality of value and importance is the point, which is made time and time again, throughout the New Testament.

It is for the value given to the whole rather than the individual believer that Paul gives such correction as found in this passage.

That such a correction has been so miss-construed is, of itself, an indication of the devil's concern that the believer should believe that God has given an abundance of gifts to His Children.

The manifold gifts of the Ministries and of the Spirit bring the presence of God in the lives of the believer to a new level of understanding and appreciation.

INTERPRETATION – V 5; *'Now I wish that you might all speak in unknown tongues. But I would rather have you prophesy. Those who prophesy are greater than those who speak in tongues, unless they interpret, so that the church may be edified.'*

As the tongue is for the personal edification of the speaker, the interruption of the tongue through an interpretation in a language which is understood by most of the hearing assembly brings edification to those who hear.

In short then, the interpretation is when a tongue, being understood as a message from God to the Church is, instructive (edified), strengthening and consoling (comforted) and or, encouraging in togetherness or like mindedness (exhorted).

The interpretation must be understandable to those who hear, otherwise it is of no benefit.:

Verse 6 -9; *'Now, brethren, if I come unto you, speaking with tongues, what shall I profit you, except I shall speak to you either by revelation, or by knowledge, or by prophesying, or by doctrine?"*

And even things without life giving sound, whether pipe or harp, except they give a distinction in the sounds, how shall it be known what is piped or harped? For if the trumpet gives an uncertain sound, who shall prepare himself to the battle?

So likewise, with you, except you utter by the tongue words easy to be understood, how shall it be known what is spoken? For you shall speak into the air.'

Tongues, on their own, do not edify the church. There must always be something to be gained, from the interaction between God and the believers, as the Body of Christ.

The gifts of Ministries and of the Spiritual Gifts, bring to bear within the congregation revelation, wisdom, teaching of the Word, comfort and knowledge and are exercised that the body corporate may both be blessed within the lives of the membership as a whole and that the Church may be a witness of the Glory of God within the community.

Paul uses the differing types of musical instruments as an example of the inter-dependency of the instruments in the performance of their respective roles, sounds.

The need for each instrument both to harmonise and synchronise so that there is understanding of the music is of paramount importance.

Paul is giving clear guidance to the Corinthian church; in that he is expressing the need that what they do – using the utterance of tongues – needs to be just as harmonised as the instruments within an orchestra.

The messages which comfort, edify and, or exhort are acceptable because they are from God and are for the benefit of the people. The golden rule is always to be observed, and it is this:

*GOD IS NOT THE AUTHOR OF CONFUSION, BUT OF DECENCY AND GOOD ORDER.

EDIFYING THE CHURCH.

Verses 10-12; *'There are, it may be, so many kinds of voices in the world, and none of them [is] without signification. Therefore, if I know not the meaning of the voice, I shall be unto him that speaks a barbarian, and he that speaks [shall be] a barbarian unto me.*

Even so, for as much as you are zealous of spiritual [gifts], seek that you may excel to the edifying of the church.'

As keen as the believers were to speak in tongues, it had no meaning or purpose, other than that of pleasing self.

I have travelled overseas, quite extensively, and have often found myself confused because I did not understand the language of the people with whom I needed to interact. I needed a Translator.

Just so within the Christian community there is the need of an interpreter. For there to be an understanding of the tongue as a gift – and it should be used sparingly – it must, as has been said before, be followed by an interpretation.

So then, Paul's injunction to the Corinthians was that if they spoke in an unknown tongue, then they should seek, and be prepared, to operate the gifting of interpretation so that the tongue may render understanding and instruction to the Body corporate.

GODLY WISDOM: Verses 14-16; *'For if I pray in an (unknown) tongue, my spirit (by the Holy Spirit that is within me), prays, but my mind is unproductive (it bears no fruit and helps nobody). Then what I am to do? I will pray with my spirit (By the Holy Spirit that is within me), but I will also pray (intelligently) with my mind and understanding.*

I will sing with my spirit (by the Holy Spirit that is within me), but I will sing (intelligently), with my mind and understanding.'

Paul identifies the difference between praying and singing in tongues which are without comprehension on the one hand and the praying and singing with comprehension on the other.

He tells us that when we pray without understanding then it is our personal spirit which prays and when we pray/sing with understanding then those around us gain blessing from the exercise.

There have been many occasions when a person has been charged, fired up, quickened if you like, by the exercising of their personal spirit through speaking in tongues, such as those suffering from brain damage etc., who have not been able to express themselves in the normal, conventional language of their understanding.

Paul tells us that this is because the unknown tongue comes from our spirit not from our intellect.

GRACE AND COMFORT:

Romans 8:26 -27; KJV. *'Likewise, the Spirit also helps our infirmities: for we know not what we should pray for as we ought: but the Spirit itself makes intercession for us with groaning which cannot be uttered.*

And he that searches the hearts knows what [is] the mind of the Spirit, because he makes intercession for the saints according to [the will of] God.

Notwithstanding that which has gone before we declare before you that praying and singing in the unknown language is of great benefit to the Christian in daily living.'

There would be many times when we just do not know what to pray, or how to express in an adequate manner those deep longings in our hearts.

There may also be times when we are asked to pray in a particular situation when we are not conversant with all the circumstances.

These are just two of the reasons why God in His infinite Wisdom has given us the capacity to pray from our spirit thus bypassing our intellect.

Paul declares that he would sing in the spirit and in his understanding, but that he would rather speak (sing) just a few words which can be understood, than thousands which of themselves have no meaningful impartation.

He goes on to qualify his ability to do this, speaking in an unknown tongue more than any of them, but puts it in perspective when he declares that it is better for the congregation to be able to give a firm Amen, which simply translated means – I Agree – than to remain ignorant of the purposes and intent of God.

*ALL GIFTS ARE FOR THE GLORY OF GOD –
NOT FOR THE GLORY OF MAN:*

Chapter Ten:
WHY TITHES & OFFERINGS?

Introduction.

Giving has always been a very sensitive subject for people to come to grips with, because it touches on the most material part of the psychology of a person's well-being: their possessions, which are very often perceived as the ultimate security.

God's heart is for us to place our security in Him. It is for this reason that we find so much about this matter in Scripture. As we study what God has to say to his people concerning tithes and offerings, we see that all material things belong to, or should we say are given to us by God in the first place.

Further to this, God, in return, expects us to return part of those material things, by faith, to Him. The most glorious thing we then discover is that God then returns to us an abundance which far surpasses the giving of our tithe and or offering.

If we are to be truly blessed in this new life in Christ Jesus, then we should come to an understanding of the basis for our tithing and our various offerings, how it should be accomplished and most importantly, what our correct attitude towards this matter should be.

God's heart is for us to place our security in him; It is for this reason that we find so much about tithes and offerings in Scripture.

It is then that we find out for ourselves the glorious truth of God's provisions for our earthly life. God returns to us an abundance which far surpasses the giving of our tithe and offering.

    1: God the Giver. We see in this chapter that God is the giver of life to all his creation.

    Genesis 2:4-23; NLT. *'This is the account of the creation of the heavens and the earth, neither wild plants nor grains were growing on the earth. For the LORD God had not yet sent rain to water the earth, and there were no people to cultivate the soil. Instead, springs came up from the ground and watered all the land.*

Then the LORD God formed the man from the dust of the ground. He breathed the breath of life into the man's nostrils, and the man became a living person.

Then the LORD God planted a garden in Eden in the east, and there he placed the man he had made. The LORD God made all sorts of trees grow up from the ground—trees that were beautiful and that produced delicious fruit. In the middle of the garden, he placed the tree of life and the tree of the knowledge of good and evil.

A river flowed from the land of Eden, watering the garden, and then dividing into four branches. The first branch, called the Pishon, flowed around the entire land of Havilah, where gold is found. The gold of that land is exceptionally pure; aromatic resin and onyx stone are also found there.

The second branch, called the Gihon, flowed around the entire land of Cush.

The third branch, called the Tigris, flowed east of the land of Asshur. The fourth branch is called the Euphrates.

The LORD God placed the man in the Garden of Eden to tend and watch over it. But the LORD God warned him, 'You may freely eat the fruit of every tree in the garden— except the tree of the knowledge of good and evil. If you eat its fruit, you are sure to die.'

Then the LORD God said, 'It is not good for the man to be alone. I will make a helper who is just right for him.'

So, the LORD God formed from the ground all the wild animals and all the birds of the sky.

He brought them to the man to see what he would call them, and the man chose a name for each one. He gave names to all the livestock, all the birds of the sky, and all the wild animals.

But still there was no helper just right for him. So, the LORD God caused the man to fall into a deep sleep. While the man slept, the LORD God took out one of the man's ribs and closed the opening.

Then the LORD God made a woman from the rib, and he brought her to the man. 'At last!' the man exclaimed. 'This one is bone from my bone, and flesh from my flesh! She will be called 'woman,' because she was taken from man. Thus, the heavens and the earth were finished, and all the host of them.

And on the seventh day God ended his work, and he rested on the seventh day from all his work which he had made. And God blessed the seventh day and sanctified it: because that in it he had rested from all his work which He had created and made.'

2. Tithing – A Definition:

The most common form of regular giving in the Bible is called tithing. This is by the giving of one (the first) tenth of the total income, to God. This is seen as a financial obligation to Him, recognising God as our principal creditor.

a. Every good thing belongs to God. We need to accept that all that we are, and consequently all that we have, is given to us by God. Tithing is a very practical way of expressing our witness to the fact that, in Him, we become very successful managers of the good things which, in His infinite wisdom, he has given us.

Psalm 24:1; *'the earth is the Lord's and everything that is in it.'* Psalm 50:10; *'every animal of the forest is mine and the cattle on a thousand hills.'* Haggai 2:8; *'the silver is mine and the gold is mine' declares the Lord Almighty.'*

The above three verses identify that the real owner of all our worldly possessions is God, and we therefore have an obligation to use His property and possessions correctly.

Consider the farmer in the field, He will remember that it is God who has given him the crops. Or consider a businessman, He will acknowledge that it is God who brings the customers. Consider an employee,

He will see that his pay envelope comes from the hand of God, not just from his employer.

If these illustrations are a correct reflection on the very nature and principle of God, then, having the mind of God and fulfilling His perfect will in our lives, we will not have any difficulty in seeing that what we tithe to God, is simply a return on His investment.

 b. The law of tithing – The principle of Grace.

Christians are no longer bound by the law handed down to Moses'. The believers in Christ, have died to it, been redeemed from it, and have become married to another, Christ Jesus our Lord – through the principle of Grace. Most of the teaching concerning the tithe is, however, found in the Old Testament, under the law.

THE MEANING OF GRACE IS:
'GOD'S RICHES AT CHRIST'S EXPENSE.

The question is this. Has the end of the law, seen the end of the tithe? To answer this question, we need to bring the Old Testament teaching into context, because:

EVERYTHING CAN BE TAKEN OUT OF CONTEXT,
AND USED AS A PRETEXT FOR ANYTHING.

 c. Pre-Mosaic: Adam, Abraham and Jacob were before the Law of Moses. Therefore, their tithing was like ours – that of the New Testament – under Grace.

Adam: God claimed man to be perfectly created.

Genesis 1: 27 & 31; *'So God created man in his [own] image, in the image of God created he him; male and female created he them. And God saw everything that he had made, and behold, [it was] very good. And the evening and the morning were the sixth day.'*

Abraham. A tenth of all he had.

Genesis 14:20; *'And blessed be the Highest God, which hath delivered thine enemies into thy hand. And he gave him tithes of all.'*

Jacob: A commitment to tithe.

Genesis 28:20-22; *'And Jacob vowed a vow, saying, If God will be with me, and will keep me in this way that I go, and will give me bread to eat, and raiment to put on, So that I come again to my father's house in peace; then shall the LORD be my God:*

And this stone, which I have set [for] a pillar, shall be God's house: and of all that you shalt give me I will surely give the tenth unto you O God.'

d: Moses: The dispensation of the law.

Joshua 1:8; *'This book of the law shall not depart out of your mouth; but you shall meditate therein day and night, that you may observe to do according to all that is written therein: for then you shall make your way prosperous, and then you shall have good success.'*

The laws contained in these books of law passed down through the generations have both a natural and spiritual application.

In the same way, the laws concerning the tithe and the offerings, as parts of the law have both natural and spiritual applications attached to them.

They are not just practical, for the ongoing work of the ministry, but they are also spiritual in that the recognition of all God's gifts is thereby rightfully ascribed to God.

Malachi: A test of His ability to give.

Malachi 3:7-12 KJV. *'Even from the days of your fathers you are gone away from my ordinances and have not kept them. Return unto me, and I will return unto you, saith the LORD of hosts. But ye said, wherein shall we return? Will a man rob God? Yet ye have robbed me. But ye say, wherein have we robbed thee? In tithes and offerings. Ye are cursed with a curse: for ye have robbed me, even this whole nation.*

Bring ye all the tithes into the storehouse, that there may be meat in mine house, and prove me now herewith, saith the LORD of hosts, if I will not open you the windows of heaven, and pour you out a blessing, that there shall not be room enough to receive it.

And I will rebuke the devourer for your sake's, and he shall not destroy the fruits of your ground; neither shall your vine cast her fruit before the time in the field, saith the LORD of hosts. And all nations shall call you blessed: for ye shall be a delight-some land, saith the LORD of hosts.'

Jesus endorses the tithe.

Matthew 23:23: *'Woe unto you, scribes and Pharisees, hypocrites! for you pay tithe of mint and anise and cumin and have omitted the weightier [matters] of the law, judgement, mercy, and faith: these ought you to have done, and not to leave the other undone.'*

In the above timeline we can see that tithing was in operation as a principle of love before the introduction of the 'Law of Moses.'

When the latter law was operating it brought with it the compulsion and a sense of clarification (legalism) which lasted until the time of Christ. Note that 'the law was until John.' Matthew 11:13 *(this was until the time of John's ministry, not at its completion).*

We have established that the tithing principle espoused in Genesis, and then taken up again with the advent of the Messiah, is in the form of 'A GRACE PRINCIPLE' and not a law of bondage.

Let me explain in the easiest way I can, for this was how I was taught.

Creation – Eden = GRACE.
    Sin – legalism = LAW.
        Jesus – Redeemer = GRACE.

We also have discovered that the tithe is a tenth part of the whole (all that we have).

3. Three Factors: concerning the tithe as applied, throughout the Word of God:

A. During the lives of Adam through Jacob inclusive, the 'Law of Moses,' was not an issue because they – the Laws of Moses – were still in the future.

B. 'Moses Law' were mostly of a carnal or material nature and significance. They were often used as band-aides to the real principles of living, Godly lives.

In this regard the Law whatever its origin is deemed to failure, because of our human frailties and limitations. This is what I call:

*MAN'S FINITE CAPACITY
IS TRYING TO COPE WITH AN INFINITE GOD.

C. Through Jesus, our Redeemer King, the principle of God's supreme love is made manifest in us. We who are the inheritors of the Kingdom can again release – by our own desire, and not under the compulsion of the law – within God's infinite love and blessings.

4. Tithing Today.

From all that we have studied so far, we see that, while tithing was a law in the Old Testament, it was built on far more than Moses' written commandments.

The law merely acknowledged the principle which was already in existence. In other words, the law of tithing brought into being by Moses, was based on the older principles of love.

We see that this stemmed from a gratitude to God and recognition that, while the 'whole' belongs to the Lord, in a special way He has reserved the 'tithes' as being 'holy.'

It has been established that the legality of the times of Moses, no longer applies because the Redeemer has come.

However, the love of Christ does, and surely has, a greater motivation and freedom than those Old Testament words cast in stone tablets. Therefore, we are encouraged in the New Testament pattern to bring our tithes and our offerings into the Lord's storehouse willingly, not under the force of Law.

5. Sowing and Reaping.

This is a spiritual principle, which, when followed with faith, produces a return on the gifts given. This is of course inevitable for, as we have already established, God is a giving God, and He is no man's debtor.

Having already considered the law (principle) of love, 'Receiving to Give.' Now we consider the second law (principle), that of sowing and reaping, 'Giving to Receive.'

Proverbs 11:24; *'One man gives freely, yet gains even more; another withholds unduly, but comes to poverty.'*

2 Corinthians 9:6; *'Whoever sows sparingly will also reap sparingly and whoever sows generously will also reap generously.'*

Luke 6:38; *'Give and it will be given to you; a good measure running over. For with the measure you use, it will be measured to you.'*

6. The Ease of Tithing.

Malachi 3:10-12; *'Bring all the tithes into the storehouse, that there may be meat in mine house, and prove me now herewith, saith the LORD of hosts, if I will not open you the windows of heaven, and pour you out a blessing, that [there shall] not [be room] enough [to receive it].*

And I will rebuke the devourer for your sakes, and he shall not destroy the fruits of your ground; neither shall your vine cast her fruit before the time in the field, said the LORD of hosts. And all nations shall call you blessed: for you shall be a delight some land, saith the LORD of hosts.'

God promises His people that He will prevent pests from devouring your crops, and the vines in your field will not cast off their fruit.

In fact, God was so bold in this promise that he said in verse 10, 'that we should bring all the tithes into the storehouse, that there may be provision in my house.'

He goes on to let us have confidence when he literally challenges us, the believer, to prove He is the 'now time' of our faith. The Lord of Hosts, 'I will open for you the windows of heaven, and pour you out a blessing, that there shall not be room enough for you to receive it.'

This Scripture is very important because it is the only time in all of God's Word, where he challenges us to test him to see not only his word but also his faithfulness, and not only his word and faithfulness, but also, and by no means least, his ability.

When we are initially faced with the issue of tithing, we are often overwhelmed with the material implications of such actions.

We can give both personal testimonies and the countless testimonies of others, of what God is able to do when we apply his principles in this area of life. Unexpected changes for the better in financial situations are more often the normal outcome. When we obey and put into practice this, one of life's mysteries to us, but unfathomable truths of a loving God. We have entered a New and Living Way.

    7. A New Creation Experience.

    2 Corinthians 5:17; *'Therefore if any man [be] in Christ, [he is] a new creature: old things are passed away; behold, all things are become new.'*

This is yet another aspect of a changed life which will flow from our compliance with God's Principles of Love. As a new creation in Christ Jesus, many of our old life patterns have changed.

Therefore, just as an example of the costing factor of the average person outside of Christ, it is most revealing to consider that a report – albeit some years ago – from the Commonwealth Bureau of Statistics, estimated that the average Australian family spends the following, as a percentage of family income in a recent sensis:

    17% gambling. 8% tobacco, alcohol.
    28% food. 37% housing

The point which we make here is that changes in spending habits, (the top two items in particular) often more than compensate for the 10% tithe which is given to God.

8. What is the Right Attitude to Riches?

3 John: 2; *'Beloved I wish above all things that you may prosper and be in health, even as your soul prospers.'*

God desires us to live in prosperity, but we must not take this message out of the context of the total Christian life. For example, there is the promise which Jesus gave to his Disciples, who had left everything,

Mark 10:28-31; *'Then Peter began to say unto him, Lo, we have left all and have followed You. And Jesus answered and said, Verily I say unto you, 'There is no man that has left house, or brethren, or sisters, or father, or mother, or wife, or children, or lands, for my sake, and the gospel's,*

But he shall receive a hundredfold now in this time, houses, and brethren, and sisters, and mothers, and children, and lands, with persecutions; and in the world to come eternal life. But many [that are] first shall be last; and the last first.'

One hundred times as much as they had forgone, in this present age, which included eternal life in the physical sense.

However, there are also the promises of persecutions along with the treasures of the kingdom.

*CHRISTIANITY IS NOT COMPLETE WITHOUT THE INDIVIDUAL PERSON TAKING UP THE CROSS.

In the New Testament there are many wealthy people whom God had blessed Nicodemus and Cornelius to name just two of them.

On the other side of the material ledger are the likes of John, a prisoner on a desolate island called Patmos, Peter, who chose to be crucified upside down, and Paul who spent so much of his time in prison.

Of these we simply know that God says in: Philippians 4:19; that He *"Met all their needs, according to his glorious riches, in Christ Jesus."*

Both riches and poverty have their respective set of problems. Most people are aware of the problems of poverty, even if they are not themselves poor.

But when we look and hear the news from around the world, and its paralysing grip on the lives of so many people, we become perplexed and in despair.

Many do not realise however, that riches can in themselves bring problems, that old saying is quite true. 'It is not that money is evil, but that the love of money tends to evil.'

The tendency to self-sufficiency without a dependence on God can become obstacles in our relationship with God and people in general.

Paul describes how to overcome those obstacles as he relates his victory over them.

Philippians 4:12-13; *'I know how to be abased and live humbly in straitened circumstances, and I know also how to enjoy plenty and live in abundance.*

I have learned in all circumstances, the secret of facing every situation, whether well fed, of going hungry, having a sufficiency and to spare or going without and being in want.

I have the strength for all things in Christ Who empowers me. I am ready for anything and equal to anything through Him, who infuses inner strength into me, that is, I am self-sufficient in Christ's sufficiency.'

1 Timothy 6:5-11; *'The perverse disputing of men of corrupt minds, and destitute of the truth, supposing that gain is godliness: from such withdraw thyself.*

But godliness with contentment is great gain. For we brought nothing into [this] world, [and it is] certain we can carry nothing out. And having food and raiment let us be therewith content. But they that will be rich fall into temptation and a snare, and [into] many foolish and hurtful lusts, which drown men in destruction and perdition.

For the love of money is the root of all evil: which while some coveted after, they have erred from the faith and pierced themselves through with many sorrows.

But you, O man of God, flee these things; and follow righteousness, godliness, faith, love, patience, meekness.'
Paul points out in this letter to Timothy, that in wealth, it is important to have the right attitude.

*'TO EXERISE *GODLINESS WITH CONTENTMENT IS GREAT GAIN.'*

God's clear intention is that we might be rich, and He has a purpose in mind for this cause.

2 Corinthians 10:11; *'You will be made rich in every way so that you can be generous on every occasion.'*

This is the correct attitude, and along with the ability to wisely manage riches, always will produce a positive outcome upon the return that God brings to tithing.

9. Tithes and Offerings: A Matter of Attitude.

Hebrews 7. shows that tithes were paid, thus implying a debt owed, whereas in 2 Corinthians 8:3; offerings were given from time to time, *'as they were able.'*

The obvious and equally important factor is that it is not the amount of the offering that was pleasing to God, but the attitude in which the offering was given:

The Widows Mite,

Luke 21:1-4; *'And Jesus looked up and saw the rich men casting their gifts into the treasury. And he saw also a certain poor widow casting into the treasury two mites.*

And he said, 'Of a truth I say unto you, that this poor widow hath cast in more than they all: For all these have of their abundance cast in unto the offerings of God: but she of her penury hath cast in all the living that she had.'

This is a good illustration that there were at least two perceptions as to the tithe. One was the rich giving out of their abundance. The other was the poor widow giving out of her means.

Unity of Purpose Producing Corporate Action.

Acts 2:44-45; *'And all that believed were together and had all things common; And sold their possessions and goods, and parted them to all [men], as every man had need.'*

Producing Provisions from The Storehouse.

Acts 11:28; *'And there stood up one of them named Agabus and signified by the Spirit that there should be great dearth throughout the entire world: which came to pass in the days of Claudius Caesar.'*

The early Christians were very spontaneous and generous in their gifts to the needy amongst them.

Acts 11:9-10; *'Then the disciples, every man according to his ability, determined to send relief unto the brethren which dwelt in Judea: Which also they did, and sent it to the elders by the hands of Barnabas and Saul.'*

10: Tithing is an Act of Grace.

2 Corinthians 8:1-5; *'Moreover, brethren, we do you to wit of the grace of God bestowed on the churches of Macedonia;*

How that in a great trial of affliction the abundance of their joy and their deep poverty abounded unto the riches of their liberality.

For to [their] power, I bear record, yes, and beyond [their] power [they were] willing of themselves;

Praying us with much entreaty that we would receive the gift, and [take upon us] the fellowship of the ministering to the saints.

And [this they did], not as we hoped, but first gave their own selves to the Lord, and unto us by the will of God.'

11: The Function & Purpose of the Tithe.

The tithe is used to support the ministry working within the Christian church (the body of Christ). The following scriptural evidence are supportive of this practice.

Tithes are, For the Work of The Body Ministry.

1 Corinthians 16:1-3; *'Now concerning the collection for the saints, as I have given order to the churches of Galatia, even so do you. Upon the first [day] of the week let every one of you lay by him in store, as [God] hath prospered him, that there be no gatherings when I come.*

And when I come, whomsoever you shall approve by [your] letters, them will I send to bring your liberality unto Jerusalem.'

Tithes Releases Worthy Ministry.

Philippians 4:10-20; *'But I rejoiced in the Lord greatly, that now at the last your care of me hath flourished again; wherein you were also careful, but you lacked opportunity. Not that I speak in respect of want for I have learned, in whatsoever state I am, [therewith] to be content. I know both how to be abased, and I know how to abound: everywhere and in all things, I am instructed both to be full and to be hungry, both to abound and to suffer need.*

*I CAN DO ALL THINGS THROUGH CHRIST WHICH STRENGTHENS ME.

Notwithstanding you have well done, that you did communicate with my affliction.

Now you Philippians know also, that in the beginning of the gospel, when I departed from Macedonia, no church communicated with me as concerning giving and receiving, but you only.

For even in Thessalonica, you sent once and again unto my necessity. Not because I desire a gift: but I desire fruit that may abound to your account.

But I have all, and abound I am full, having received of Epaphroditus the things [which were sent] from you, an odour of a sweet smell, a sacrifice acceptable, well pleasing to God.

But my God shall supply all your need according to his riches in glory by Christ Jesus. Now unto God and our Father [be] glory for ever and ever. Amen.'

Tithes Relieve Material Worries.

1 Corinthians 9:3-14; '*Mine answer to them that do examine me is this: Have we not power to eat and to drink? Have we not power to lead about a sister, a wife, as well as other apostles, and [as] the brethren of the Lord, and Cephas? Or I only and Barnabas, have not we power to forbear working?*

Who goes war faring any time at his own charges? Who plants a vineyard, and eats not of the fruit thereof? Who feeds a flock, and eats not of the milk of the flock?

Say I these things as a man? or said not the law the same also?

For it is written in the law of Moses, You, shalt not muzzle the mouth of the ox that treads out the corn. Does God take care for oxen? said He, [it] altogether for our sake's?

For our sake's, no doubt, [this] is written, that those who plough, should plough in hope; and that he that threshes in hope, should be partaker of his hope.

If we have sown unto you, spiritual things, [is it] a great thing if we shall reap your carnal things?

If others be partakers of [this] power over you, [are] not we rather? Nevertheless, we have not used this power; but suffer all things, lest we should hinder the gospel of Christ.

Do you not know that they which minister about holy things live [of the things] of the temple? and they which wait at the altar are partakers with the altar? Even so has the Lord ordained that they which preach the gospel should live of the gospel.'

Tithes are Worthy Recompense.

Timothy 5:17-18; *'Let the elders that rule well be counted worthy of double honour, especially they who labour in the word and doctrine. For the scripture says, Thou shalt not muzzle the ox that treads out the corn. And the labourer [is] worthy of his reward.'*

Cheerful In Our Giving.

2 Corinthians 9:7; *'Every man according as he purposes in his heart, [so let him give]; not grudgingly, or of necessity: for God loves a cheerful giver.'*

Each Christian should give accordingly with a heart to give, not reluctantly or under compulsion, for God loves a cheerful giver. It follows directly from the law of love we have dealt with earlier in this study.

Our giving is a measure of the quality that stems from the spiritual life within us and our love towards God.

12: Giving is from the whole.

Matthew 25:34-40; *'Then shall the King say unto them on his right hand, Come, you blessed of my Father, inherit the kingdom prepared for you from the foundation of the world:*

For I was hungry, and you gave me meat: I was thirsty, and you gave me drink: I was a stranger, and you took me in: Naked, and you clothed me: I was sick, and you visited me: I was in prison, and you came unto me.

Then shall the righteous answer him, saying, Lord, when saw we you hungry, and fed [you]? or thirsty, and gave [you] drink? When saw we you a stranger, and took [you] in? or naked, and clothed [you]? Or when saw we you sick, or in prison, and came unto you?

And the King shall answer and say unto them, Verily I say unto you, in as much as you have done [it] unto one of the least of these my brethren, you have done [it] unto me.'

We are exhorted on many occasions, to give substances other that money, to those in need. The needs of people are far greater than just financial and where we can meet that need, whatever it may be, we are encouraged to do so.

13: Common-sense Is Godly Wisdom.

A continual task of 'Fulfilling Your Potential,' is the achieving of a balance between faith and common-sense and is always prudent good management.

Both need to be activated as normal practice, so that God's richest blessing can be poured out through our daily living. The following are the guidelines which I believe God has set before us and therefore are given as a principled method of being secure in the process.

A. It is unwise to write a cheque when there are insufficient funds to cover it.

B. A Christian person deeply in debt, should give that debt a priority before making significant offerings.

C. Six practical laws of thrift need to be observed.

    1) Avoid impulse buying.

    2) Keep a record of all your expenditure as a control.

    3) Formulate a practical budget.

    4) Do not be pressured by either your peers or by advertising gimmick

    5) Always remember that bargains are only bargains if they are needed.

    6) Do not borrow for non-capital items.

D. There are two plans – that together – embrace God's Divine Pattern for Our Living.

    1: God, Roof, Food, Clothes, Household Bills, and Pleasures:

    2: God, Self, Spouse, Children, Work, Church, Pleasures

Warning: I have found there are those who place church in a higher position than that which I have listed above, however God's plan, as above, values places family as the sovereign entity. When placing Church matters above the needs of the family unit, we have no witness worthy of the Lord's name.

Money and possessions at first glance would seem to be far from spiritual things. A closer look reveals that they are all from the hand of God and for our benefit and usage.

In tithing we apply God's divine plan for our prosperity and well-being.

In giving, we activate a dynamic principle, by which God can supernaturally bless us even further.

When we understand practice, and develop His principle, the same attitude towards possessions and giving that our Heavenly Father has, it is then, that He will pour out His abundant blessings upon us.

As you the believer come to the end of this set of studies, I assure you that my thoughts and prayers are with you.

As your continual pursuit of the things of Jesus Christ, brings within you the desire to be ambassadors, to a world who needs to come to Him who gave His all for them who do not yet know Him.

I pray that you will have gained a more rounded understanding of this subject, 'Fulfilling Your Potential in Christ' and that God may continue to encourage your use of those gifts as there is need of them.

P.B.

Thank you for purchasing 'Fulfilling Your Potential in Christ' This is my sixth book and is a compilation of the last 50 years in which I have been blessed to lead new Christians into an understanding – and with the Holy Spirit's guidance – engage them to pursue the victorious life that God has promised to all who believe, in Him.

I hope – with Anticipated Expectation – that you prayerfully gain something from its pages.

REQUEST FOR YOUR CONSIDERATION:

'Point 2 Point with Jesus' is a Christian Ministry dedicated to raise ministries wherever God directs. To do this we need funding and respectfully ask you the reader to give consideration in support, through donations, so that we can support such potential ministries, and equip them for service. Of course, your Prayerful support is also a blessing in all we do, and to Him we give all Glory and Honour. AMEN.

This book and others to follow will help service the "Core" working of our ministry.

The author's other books available for the reader:

'Living in Faith.' … 'Our God of Common-Sense.' … 'Living in the Way, the Truth, and the Life.' … 'Walking in the Light of God's Word' … 'The Foundation for Christian Living.' … 'Christian Leadership Principles & Teamwork in the Local Fellowship.' … 'Jesus: The Personal Son of God' … 'Getting Rid of Stinking Thinking.' …

All finances gained from the purchase of this, and other 'Point 2 Point With Jesus' enterprises will be sown into the work of Acts 29ers International Ministries, an affiliated member with both the ACM and ACMI accredited Christian Bodies.

Our bank details for donations are as follows:
BSB 633 111000 Acc Number 22 988 0083

     Thanking God for your considerations.
            P.B. 2025.

Commendation:

Barrie presents as a man of great integrity and enthusiasm. He is dynamic in his evangelistic endeavours and demonstrates a diverse, flexible yet empathetic disposition.

He has great insight and understanding of the vast needs encountered across the many cultures within our nation. He is an encouraging man with a great love for God and His people. He offers many years of experience in teaching, preaching and the sharing of practical biblical principles with individuals who are seeking purpose and fulfilment through relationship and guidance, all with an ongoing holistic development in an often seemingly difficult life and times. His inspired writings have been instrumental in the releasing of people from despair, depression, grief, drug dependencies, anxiety and much more. It is his heart's desire to assist people through the 'Common-sense Teachings' found in the Scriptures, finding new hope and joy in the search for answers to life's questions and more.

The Lord has given Barrie an apostolic anointing along with a specific word of encouragement, which in short tells us that "Books are for reading, but without understanding they are just words."

In his new role as a 'RE-TYRED MINISTER, Barrie is equipped by the Holy Spirit and ready for God's work and God's people. We commend this book to the reader as an example of the common-sense approach which Barrie brings to those who like reading and understanding the Good News of Jesus and His heavenly Father.

Noelene D. Rowland-Hornblow

Printed by Libri Plureos GmbH in Hamburg, Germany